Dick Clark's
AMERICAN
BANDSTAND

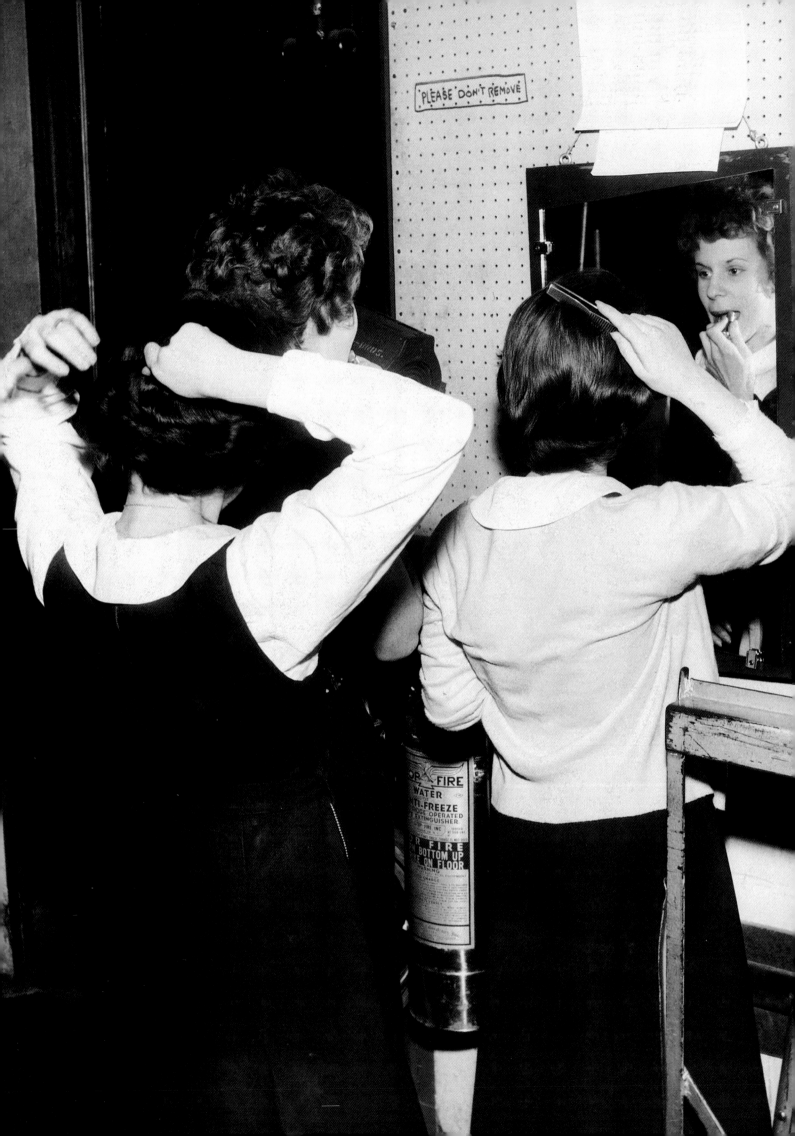

Dick Clark's
AMERICAN
BANDSTAND

TEXT BY DICK CLARK WITH FRED BRONSON
CAPTIONS BY RAY SMITH

CollinsPublishers
A Division of HarperCollinsPublishers

CONTENTS

Let The Good Times Roll 12

Hard Day's Night 80

Disco Fever 120

We Got The Beat 152

Acknowledgments And Photography Credits 186

Index 188

After waiting outside on Market Street in the heat and cold and rain, kids lucky enough to get into American Bandstand were anxious and excited. Walking through the doors to Philadelphia's WFIL-TV's Studio B, where teenage life and music were all-important, was like walking into Oz. The lights, cameras, and music made the studio a magical place; there was, as with any television show, a lot of illusion. Television was still a relatively new medium in 1957, and the studio was crude by today's standards. The cameras and lights were large, bulky, and hard to move, making trick shots of kids dancing virtually impossible. The studio was cold, the lights were hot, the music was loud, and the floor was hard. Girls wore sneakers or flat shoes to save their feet from soreness from the cement floor. But the kids were oblivious to physical discomfort; they were the stars of the first TV show to feature real teenagers.

LET THE GOOD TIMES ROLL

I'll never forget July 9, 1956. When I went to work that morning at the WFIL studios in Philadelphia, I thought I would be doing what I did every weekday —hosting my afternoon radio show. But the general manager of WFIL-TV, George Koehler, had a surprise for me, one that changed my life forever. George said he wanted me to become the permanent host of the station's daily dance show, *Bandstand*. And, he wanted me to start that same day. I had barely gotten over the shock of the sudden promotion from radio disc jockey to television host when the studio was besieged by an angry crowd of students with picket signs. They were mad because I was replacing the previous *Bandstand* host, Bob Horn. I understood their rage, but I had nothing to do with Horn leaving the show. He was dismissed after getting in trouble with the law. Horn had never related that well to the kids on the show, but he was the captain of the ship, and the kids who danced on the show felt their destinies were in his hands. Suddenly, there I was running the show—a relatively unknown twenty-six-year-old guy who didn't even know the dancers' names.

We were minutes away from going on the air live when I walked outside to confront the two dozen picketers, furiously waving their signs. "I'm Dick Clark. I've got the job as the new host of *Bandstand*." There was no response, so I continued. "I know how you felt about Bob, but there's nothing anybody can do about it. I know he was your friend. I hope you don't dislike me because I was chosen to replace him." More silence. "I've got to get to work now. If you want to come in, please do." I went back inside. No one followed. With two minutes to go, producer Tony Mammarella gave me the good news; the kids had dropped their picket signs and come into the studio. I had survived my first crisis as the host of *Bandstand*.

Most people don't realize that before *American Bandstand* was a national phenomenon, it was a local radio show first broadcast in 1952. *Bob Horn's Bandstand* was a top-rated program on WFIL radio when Horn was asked to host a new afternoon TV series. He took the name *Bandstand* with him, but instead of playing records, he played short, filmed musical performances by artists like Peggy Lee, Nat King Cole, and George Shearing. That format was soon dropped in favor of kids dancing to the latest hit records of a new beat that had captured America. It was called rock 'n' roll, a melding of rhythm and blues, country and western, and pop music, and it was driven by guitars, drums, and percussive instruments. I don't think any of us who were there in the earliest days of rock 'n' roll had any idea that it would be more than a passing fad. Certainly people would have laughed if you had suggested that rock music would be a multi-billion dollar industry still going strong forty years later,

we shall overcome

In 1954, the Supreme Court ruled that separate schools did not mean equal education. This helped launch the civil rights movement. For many Americans it was a hard pill to swallow; white picketers armed themselves with signs, sticks, and bottles. Black activists, like the people (opposite) demonstrating in 1962 in Times Square for the release of Martin Luther King Jr. from jail, took their cause to the streets. Teens were often at the center of civil rights activity. In 1957, in Little Rock, Arkansas, Governor Orval Faubus ordered the National Guard to block nine black students from entering Central High School. President Eisenhower retaliated by ordering Federal troops to escort the kids into the school. Rock 'n' roll, closely identified with blacks and black music, also took direct hits from racists who threatened both radio stations that played the music and record stores that sold it.

or that it would become a cornerstone of American culture that would capture the imaginations of people worldwide. Today, most Americans have grown up with rock 'n' roll. The music you loved when you were a teenager still provides a touchstone to your memories. All you have to do is hear the song that was playing on the radio when you had your first date, that melancholic number that comforted you during your first break-up, or that tune that reminded you of a special friend who'd moved far away, and you're back in your teens, remembering the good old days.

American Bandstand provided the soundtrack for many people growing up, and I'm grateful to have been a part of rock 'n' roll from the beginning right up to today. I'm also thankful that *Bandstand* has given me personal relationships with the artists, songwriters, producers, and record label executives responsible for making the music. During the years I hosted the show, I was too busy to stop and think about what it all meant. This is one of the first opportunities I've had to reminisce about the people who produced, watched, and appeared on *American Bandstand* through four decades of ever-changing social mores and popular entertainment.

I wasn't that knowledgeable about rock 'n' roll when I first became the host of *Bandstand*, because I hadn't been allowed to play rock on my radio show. I had to stick to "adult" pop music, playing songs by artists like Perry Como and Rosemary Clooney. But hosting *Bandstand* was like taking a crash course in a new culture. I learned quickly—not just the facts about the music—but genuinely to love the music. During the first few weeks, Tony Mammarella picked all the songs that we played on the show. As I became more familiar with the artists and the music, I didn't have to rely on Tony so much to select the records. We soon got to the point where we would alternate— one day he would pick the music and the next day I would make the selection.

There weren't a lot of places on national television where you could watch this new phenomenon called rock 'n' roll. You could hear the new beat on a few radio stations, but if you wanted to see kids doing new dances to the sound, or artists performing the latest hits, *Bandstand* was just about your only choice. Remember, when I became the host of the local *Bandstand* show in 1956, rock 'n' roll had only been in the mainstream for a year. It evolved from rhythm and blues, especially the big band jump music of the forties, as performed by Louis Jordan ("Five Guys Named Moe" (1941), "Saturday Night Fish Fry" (1949)). The people who keep track of rock history can't agree on what the first rock 'n' roll record was, although the leading candidate is "Rocket 88" by Jackie Brenston & His Delta Cats, a 1951 recording that featured a very young Ike Turner. One thing people do agree on, though, is that the first rock song that went to number one was "Rock Around the Clock" by Bill Haley & His Comets. The single topped the charts for the first time on July 9, 1955, one year to the day before I first hosted *Bandstand*.

Rock music had plenty of detractors. That may be difficult to believe today, when rock 'n' roll is so pervasive in our culture, but in the fifties a lot of people were afraid of the music. Some of their fears were based on racial prejudices. Religious leaders spoke out against rock 'n' roll because of puritanical beliefs. Some of the more extreme religious figures arranged record burnings to "save" their young flocks from Satan. The term "rock and roll" was a euphemism for sexual intercourse. When the Dominoes sang about rock and roll in their 1951 recording "Sixty-Minute Man," they weren't referring to music. Neither were the Clovers in their 1952 single, "Ting-A-Ling." Politicians spoke out against rock 'n' roll, too. Even people in the recording industry, like the Columbia Records head of artists and repertoires, "Sing-A-Long" bandleader Mitch Miller, condemned it. I bet none of them could have predicted we would come to regard rock 'n' rollers as artists, worthy of presidential honors, or visit museums full of rock memorabilia, and that each ensuing generation would embrace this music as its own.

I didn't realize it at the time, but because most adults were so busy putting down rock 'n' roll, it wasn't very long before I, as a young adult, was recognized as a champion of the new music. Most television shows shunned rockers like Gene Vincent ("Be-Bop-A-Lula" (1955)), Eddie Cochran ("Summertime Blues" (1958)), and Duane Eddy ("Beause They're Young" (1960)) or treated them as novelties. *Bandstand*—and I, by association—embraced them. Elvis Presley appeared in prime time because his immense popularity guaranteed high ratings, but if you wanted to see Chuck Berry, Jerry Lee Lewis, Buddy Holly, or Fats Domino, you watched *American Bandstand*. All of them, like hundreds of other artists, made their first television appearances on the show. As a result, *Bandstand* conferred a mainstream respectability on the artists and their music that they couldn't get from being heard on the radio.

As important as the artists and music were, one of the elements most responsible for the long-lasting success of *American Bandstand* was the kids who danced on the shows. All over the

THE MOST EFFECTIVE WAY TO FIGHT COMMUNISM IS TO LEARN ALL YOU CAN ABOUT IT.

red scare

In February 1950, Wisconsin Senator Joseph McCarthy offhandedly claimed he had a list of 205 Communists working in the U.S. State Department. For the rest of the decade, Americans obsessed about routing out Communists who threatened the American "way of life." According to McCarthy and his supporters, Communists were everywhere—in our homes, schools, work places, and the entertainment industry. "Commies," they said, were making movies, writing plays, teaching children, and running our government. Warnings to watch out for Communists were everywhere, including comic strips (above). In the Communist witch hunt that McCarthy provoked, reason was abandoned, careers ruined, and lives destroyed. For some Americans, rock 'n' roll was an assault just as dangerous as Communism.

country, teenagers rushed home from school to watch other teenagers do the newest dances, wear the hippest fashions, and rub shoulders with the most popular artists of the day. Watching *Bandstand* was like having a window onto a daily party that let you in on the latest trends and music. Most importantly, it was a show specifically designed for teenagers.

People always ask if I was nervous the first day I hosted *Bandstand*. I can honestly say I wasn't. I was comfortable in a studio from nine years of working on TV in Utica, New York, and Philadelphia, not to mention the numerous beer commercials I did for wrestling shows. Some people think I was born with a microphone in my hand, and my wife says I'm more

at ease in a TV studio than in social situations. Besides, nothing about the show was changed other than the host. The sets were the same, the crew was the same, and we continued popular spots such as Rate-A-Record, Spotlight Dance, and Roll Call. It was important for me to have Tony Mammarella on my side; he had wanted to be the new permanent host of the show, and I wasn't sure how he would feel about me getting the job. But, he made it a point the first day to let me know we would be working as a team, and I appreciated that.

Those were great times, our first year at WFIL. We were on the air live every weekday afternoon from 2:30 until 5:30, playing all the hits, from "The

tube time

After decades of deprivation during the Great Depression and World War II, Americans in the postwar years finally had money to spend and innovative things to buy, especially televisions (above). Between 1946, when RCA first introduced TV for mass consumption, and 1952, the number of television sets in use went from 6,000 to 20,000,000. People loved the fact that for the first time in history they could see the world from the comfort of their own living rooms. Actually, the shows they were seeing in those early years were visual versions of what they had been listening to on radio during the thirties and forties: Burns & Allen, Amos 'n' Andy, Our Miss Brooks, and Jack Benny. Even American Bandstand was modeled on Philadelphia's WPEN Radio's 950 Club, a popular radio dance show.

Wayward Wind" by Gogi Grant to "Green Door" by Jim Lowe. The year 1956 was a watershed year for music; even though Bill Haley and Elvis Presley reached the top of the charts, much of the music on the radio was still pop, not rock. By the end of the year, Fats Domino's "Blueberry Hill" and Ivory Joe Hunter's "Since I Met You Baby" were big hits, alongside pop songs like "Hey, Jealous Lover" by Frank Sinatra, "True Love" by Bing Crosby and Grace Kelly, and "Mama From the Train" by Patti Page. It was a transition period, and *Bandstand* made its own contribution, playing *all* of the hits on the charts.

Our starting time of 2:30 P.M. was governed by how fast the kids could get to the studio once school

was over. The kids came mostly from two high schools, West Catholic and South Philadelphia. Our studio was crude by today's standards, but not bad for a city the size of Philadelphia in the fifties. The crew didn't only work on our show—they'd finish the cooking show next door and have thirty or forty seconds to run to our set. We had three huge black and white cameras. If I wanted to talk to the control room, I called them on a telephone from the podium. It was a real working phone, not a prop, but like the podium and the Rate-A-Record board, it became one of the recognizable features of the show that helped make *Bandstand* a familiar, welcome visitor in millions of homes across America. Still, *Bandstand* at this point was local. But, I was ambitious and didn't plan to let the show or my career stagnate. With its universal appeal to teenagers, I thought *Bandstand* could be even bigger. There was no reason that the same things that attracted kids in Philadelphia couldn't attract kids all over the country. I believed *Bandstand* belonged on the network.

Part of my inspiration came from the strong sense of self-preservation I've always had. WFIL was an ABC affiliate, and when the network announced plans to replace an afternoon movie slot with a new show, it urged its affiliates to carry whatever that new show might be. I was afraid WFIL was going to drop our local program for what the network was going to offer, even though Tony assured me we were too profitable to be canceled. Since Tony had been approached by five local program directors to find out how to do a *Bandstand*-type show in their local markets, I thought we could be the replacement show. I wanted Ted Fetter, program director of ABC in New York, to get a look at our show. This was long before videotape and satellite broadcasting, and the only way to make a copy of a television show was to film it off the air. We had a kinescope made for Fetter, but I found out the network brass already had one of the show and had watched it more than once. They promised to get back to us.

In the middle of June 1957, I was on vacation visiting my parents in Utica. Everyday I called my secretary Marlene to see if we'd heard from the network. On June 19, she told me that I'd received a "don't call us, we'll call you" letter from Fetter, polite but nothing more. In my naiveté, I thought he meant it when he said, "If you are ever in New York, why don't you drop in and say hello." Since I was in New York—New York state—I flew to Manhattan and begged Fetter to give *Bandstand* a try on the network. He didn't say yes that day, but a month later, he called to say that he and network head Jim Aubrey would pay us a visit in Philadelphia. Three days after they'd seen the show in person, Fetter phoned to tell me that ABC liked us enough to give the show a four-week trial. The only changes would be a new set, different lighting, and a slight change of name. On August 5, 1957, the nation got its first look at *American Bandstand*.

If you were living in Philadelphia, the show looked and sounded like the same old *Bandstand*, thanks to Tony Mammarella. The network executives had come up with a list of "improvements" they wanted to make, like having the kids wear make-up, applauding at the end of each record, and showing photos of artists while we were playing their songs. Tony kept his cool but he was angry at the network's suggestions—after all, *Bandstand* was an incredibly successful local show. He didn't think it needed to be changed. Realizing Tony's anger, Aubrey had the good sense to take him aside and ask him what shouldn't be changed. Tony replied—the music, the dancing, and Dick Clark.

On *American Bandstand*, we presented all kinds of music, but to this day I still hear the criticism that we favored the white artists who recorded pop versions of rhythm and blues songs over the black artists who recorded the original versions. It was never true. I may have kicked off our very first network show by playing Jerry Lee Lewis' "Whole Lot of Shakin' Going On," but one of the guests that day was Billy Williams, a rhythm and blues singer who crossed over to the pop charts with "I'm Gonna Sit Right Down and Write Myself a Letter." The other guest act was the Chordettes, a white pop female singing group famous for "Mr. Sandman." Before the year was out, our guests included other black R&B artists, like Jackie Wilson, Chuck Berry, the Bobbettes, and the Five Satins. We also introduced pop and country performers like Buddy Holly & the Crickets, Bobby Darin, Gene Vincent, Webb Pierce, Johnny Mathis, and two boys from New York named Tom & Jerry, who would later use their real names: Simon & Garfunkel.

Philadelphia was home to a lot of talented artists, songwriters, and producers. Our first-year guests also included Danny & the Juniors, a group of high school students who sang on street corners before going to number one with "At the Hop" (1958), and the popular Philadelphia artist Frankie Avalon, a teenager who played trumpet before he hit it big with "Venus" (1959). Over the years, we presented a lot of hometown folks—Chubby Checker, Bobby Rydell, Fabian, Dee Dee Sharp, the Orlons, and the Dovells. Critics who asked why we used so many local acts didn't realize we were booking ten acts a week on one show, and later, five acts a week on my Saturday night prime time show from New York. That's fifteen artists a week. Often someone would cancel at the last minute. All we had to do was pick up the phone and call someone from South Philadelphia and they were at the studio quickly to fill in for someone who couldn't show up from California.

The city was also home to a lot of people in the record business. I remember Dave Miller, who owned Essex Records and who started the "101 Strings" concept. He was a genius when it came to business, and he built a multi-million dollar company, starting with Bill Haley & His Comets. Then there was Bernie

Lowe, who played piano for bandleader Paul Whiteman. Bernie had a great eye for talent and signed artists like Charlie Gracie and Bobby Rydell, and later on, Chubby Checker. Bernie's company was Cameo-Parkway, one of the legendary record companies of rock 'n' roll's early days. And, there was a piano teacher named Artie Singer, who started Singular Records and had a major hit with "At the Hop" by Danny & the Juniors. These were the pioneer days of the modern recording industry, when the key word in "music business" was music, not business. Record labels were small, independent companies, often staffed by family members, friends, or a handful of employees. The people who started these labels were passionate about the music. Today, there are six global conglomerates that dominate the business, and they are frequently run by lawyers and business affairs people who are more concerned about the bottom line than about the music.

Our doors were always open to representatives from the record labels who wanted to convince us to play their latest releases or book their newest artists. Most of these people were honest, hard-working and fun to be with. One who has remained a friend to this day is Red Schwartz, a man who started out selling Chevrolets. He was a high school friend of Tony's, and after Tony went into TV, Red became the second most popular R&B disc jockey in town, on WDAS-AM. Red had a great ear, and if he said a record was going to be a smash, it usually was. After he became a record label promotion rep, I wouldn't always jump on his records. I was reluctant to play "Book of Love" by the Monotones because I thought it was a novelty song with limited appeal. One day Red took the unusual step of popping into my tiny office with the group in tow. He put the record on and had them lip synch to it, and I was finally convinced the song could be a hit—in fact, I said we'd put the group on the show that day. Then Red told me, "Dick, they're not the Monotones. They're five kids I picked up in the street and rehearsed for a day and a half." That was typical of Red. But I did end up playing the song on the show, and Red was right— "Book of Love" was a top five hit in 1958.

A couple months later, Red was working for Vee Jay Records in Chicago when he dropped by our office. He picked up the music playlist of songs we had set for *Bandstand* that day, and without asking anyone, crossed off a song and added the record he was pushing. "Hey, what are you doing?" I yelled at him. I told him he should at least let me hear the record first. "If you hear it, so what?" Red replied. "You'll say it stinks. Just play it on the show." I listened to it first anyway, and it sounded like a funeral dirge. But, I agreed to play "For Your Precious Love" by Jerry Butler & the Impressions on the show that day. Red was so excited he called his office in Chicago to tell them to watch *American Bandstand*. "For Your Precious Love" was played on the show, and the single went to number eleven on the Billboard chart. I still cherish those days, because it was such an innocent time.

The kids who danced on the show probably didn't think so back then, but they were more innocent, too. These were the Eisenhower years, and while some politicians today romanticize the era, it *was* a different time. Did the dancers have some of the same problems that today's teens have to cope with? Yes, but they didn't talk about them. Were they having sex? I'm sure some were, but that wasn't talked about either. While teenagers in the fifties didn't have to face life-and-death issues when dealing with sexuality like they do today, they did have to be concerned with pregnancy and contracting social diseases. If any of the girls who danced on the show got pregnant, I never knew about it. Of course, they wouldn't have told me about it anyway.

Another thing we didn't talk about in the fifties was sexual orientation. Yes, some of the kids on the show were gay, but like most aspects of sexuality, it wasn't something that was discussed publicly. On the air, we couldn't even mention the words "going steady" or say that someone had gotten "pinned." Censors feared such expressions might indicate that a boy and a girl were more than just friends, that they might be sleeping together. We used code words—for example it was all right for me to ask if a couple was

there she is

For millions of Americans, Marilyn Van Debur, Miss America 1958 (right), symbolized all that was right with America's youth. Van Debur was wholesome, perky, and feminine, the American ideal for women in the fifties. The Miss America Pageant began in 1921 as a gimmick, but once the contest was broadcast on television in 1955 it became one of America's most sacred and closely followed annual rituals. President Richard M. Nixon said it was the only television show he let daughters Julie and Tricia watch.

"going together." Remember, a lot of parents didn't even like the idea that kids were dancing together!

Two things that were forbidden in the studio were alcohol and cigarettes. If the kids did drink or smoke, they did it out of my sight. I wasn't a puritan myself—in those days I smoked and drank. But, given the criticism hurled at rock 'n' roll, the kids on *Bandstand* had to have a certain image if the show was going to succeed. There was no question that if everything about *American Bandstand* wasn't neat and scrubbed, the show wouldn't have survived its early days. We enforced a strict dress code, too. The boys had to wear jackets and ties, and the girls had to wear dresses. Tight sweaters, pants, and low necklines were verboten. Maybe some people hated rock 'n' roll, but they couldn't say the teenagers dancing on the *Bandstand* looked like juvenile delinquents—you know, wearing leather jackets or white t-shirts with packs of cigarettes rolled up in the sleeves.

The music was also made presentable, which explains why a lot of adults enjoyed watching the show. How could parents complain about their sons and daughters enjoying rock 'n' roll if squeaky clean Dick Clark endorsed it? Listening to the music was something parents and children could do together when they watched *American Bandstand*. And, by playing the music and featuring the artists on television, I helped give rock 'n' roll a credibility it didn't get by being played on the radio. If a large corporation like ABC Television could devote two-and-a-half hours of its afternoon schedule to this music, then parents could reason that it must be worthwhile. These tactics helped keep rock 'n' roll alive. But, I was not being a saint; my livelihood was at stake, too. I had a family, and I needed to keep the money coming in so I could put food on the table.

There was one important change that Tony and I made in 1957. Up until that time, the dancers on *Bandstand* had one thing in common—they were all white. You didn't see a lot of black people on TV in the fifties, or other minorities, either. This was eight years before Bill Cosby starred with Robert Culp in *I Spy*, nine years before Nichelle Nichols was cast as Lieutenant Uhura in *Star Trek*, and eleven years before Diahann Carroll played *Julia*, all pioneering roles for black actors. Even in 1968, when Petula Clark kissed Harry Belafonte on the cheek, there was an uproar among advertisers and stations in the South.

So in 1957, we were charting new territory. I don't think of myself as a hero or civil rights activist for integrating the show; it was simply the right thing to do.

19

round and round

In 1958, two businessmen figured out how to turn fifteen million pounds of a new, cheap, flexible high-density plastic into a twirling toy that caught the fancy of millions of Americans. Pricing them for under two dollars, the manufacturer, Wham-O, sold thirty million hula hoops in six months. Baby boomers—by their sheer numbers (seventy-six million by 1964)—were an economic force that bought up millions of plastic toys—model soldiers, airplanes, dolls, pop beads, Frisbees. The new toy was physical fun; it foreshadowed dance movements that would ready teenagers for the Twist, and pre-dated the aerobic craze that boomers would flock to in the eighties.

One reason I might have been sensitive to racial issues is that I was involved in the music industry, which in many ways was an integrated business. Even though I grew up in a white, Anglo-Saxon Protestant family and lived in the suburbs, I was working with many black record executives and artists. I became friends with a lot of them: some of them were uneducated people, some were poor, and many were struggling to get ahead. One artist who became more than a casual acquaintance was Sam Cooke. We had dinner together and our families socialized. He would discuss things that were wrong with American society, things that as

a white man I had never experienced. You knew that people of color faced prejudice every day of their lives, but Sam was the first person to really tell me about it in personal terms.

Later, I had a chance to experience what Sam was telling me about firsthand. In 1958, we did a live television show at the Atlanta Fairgrounds. Among the artists we booked were Conway Twitty, Joni James, Danny & the Juniors, and Sam Cooke. When we got to Atlanta, the producer of the show, Deke Heyward, told me this was the first-ever integrated show at the fairgrounds, and that we had received threatening phone calls and letters, including some from people who identified themselves as members of the Ku Klux Klan. The National Guard was called in to protect us, even though some people warned us that there were KKK members in the Guard. Deke's strategy was to lower the tension by bringing in a group of black nuns, wearing their habits, to sit primly in the front row. They had a calming effect on everybody. Backstage, I asked a concerned Sam Cooke how he felt. "I'm only going out there for three minutes," he told me. "You've got to do the whole show. How do *you* feel?" I said, "Well, if you're going on, I'm going on." Looking back on it, I don't know if courage or stupidity got me out on that stage. It probably had more to do with the old adage, "the show must go on." It did, and I'm glad to say nothing went wrong.

Philadelphia in the mid-fifties was one of the northernmost "southern" cities around. We didn't have "colored" men's rooms or signs that said "For Negroes Only," like you saw in the old days, but blacks and whites didn't hang out or party together either. It's no surprise that *Bandstand* was an exclusively white show from its beginnings with Bob Horn in 1952 to 1957. When Tony and I made the decision to bring in black dancers, no one had told us we had to, and we didn't make a big deal out of it. We found some black teenagers who wanted to dance on the show and invited them to the studio. The black guys danced with the black girls and the white guys danced with the white girls—network television wasn't ready for anything more at that point.

I remember the first time we had a black teenager take part in Rate-A-Record. If I've ever gotten nervous on television, that was the day. I was worried about what the reaction would be in the deep South. Would some ABC affiliates drop the show? The extraordinary thing was that there was absolutely no reaction—which was terrific. There were no complaints from affiliates, no letters from outraged viewers. Not one. And, our mail averaged over 20,000 letters per week! Had there been an intense negative reaction, I don't know if I would have been brave enough to expand our integration of the show. After that initial step, which was probably the single most socially significant thing we ever did on *Bandstand*, we invited more black kids to come on the show. Years later, James Avery, who played Wil Smith's Uncle Phillip on *Fresh Prince of Bel Air*, told me that the first time he ever saw a black couple dancing on television was on *American Bandstand*. Later, after the show moved to California in 1964, we included other minorities on the show, but at that point the whole issue was no big deal. Although the show was integrated, it still took years for one of the black dancers to become as famous as a white dancer. Oddly, his name was Famous Hooks, and he became a regular in the sixties when we moved the show to California.

Way before Famous, the kids on *American Bandstand* became as well-known as the artists who performed on the show. It was an incredible phenomenon. These were average teenagers from Philadelphia who never planned to pursue a career that could bring them fame. But, just by showing up at WFIL's Studio B every day to dance on the show, they became famous all over the country. Teenagers fell in love with these dancers, and wrote them tons of fan letters. They were featured in the teen magazines, and their fans kept scrapbooks full of clippings. Lots of people photographed them right off the television screen, and to this day I still get pictures in the mail that were snapped off TV sets.

The regular dancers were invited to be on the Committee, which meant they had a special card they showed our doorman, affectionately known as Bob

the Cop. That got them right in to the studio without waiting in line. This also gave us some assurance that no matter what, we would have a core group of dancers every day, and it gave the show continuity. One memorable day on *American Bandstand* in the fifties was the day no one showed up. I've carried that nightmare with me ever since. There was a snow storm *and* a rail strike, so only a few people could actually get to the studio. We took the cameras outside and played in the snow throwing snowballs at each other in the parking lot of WFIL. We filled the time with anything we could conjure up, and eventually more of the regulars showed up and saved the day. People in Phoenix and Miami thought it was amazing.

These Philadelphia kids had their moment in the sun years before Andy Warhol predicted that everyone would experience fifteen minutes of fame. For Bob Clayton and Justine Carelli, for Kenny Rossi and Arlene Sullivan, and for the other dancers, those fifteen minutes have lasted a long, long time. Even though they're now middle-aged adults, they are still recognized, and people do remember their names. Recently, I was in Atlantic City when a woman riding behind me on an escalator asked if I knew who she was. "Yes, you're Mary Elizabeth DiPiano. I drove you home after a piece of scenery fell on you." Mary didn't realize why I never forgot that day. I had insisted on driving her home to Drexel Hill so her mother could make sure she was alright. At the time, I didn't know if it was a smart thing to do, since there were just the two of us in the car, although I was happily married and knew that I had no inclination to stray. It all turned out well, and Mary was delighted that I remembered her, but corrected me on one point. "Yes, well, that was my *old* name." She was happily married, too.

If the kids who danced on the show were one of the main ingredients that kept *American Bandstand* cooking, the other was the roster of performers. For most rock 'n' roll artists, *Bandstand* was the only network TV show that would book them. One of our most frequent early guests was Antoine Fats Domino, an artist who helped put New Orleans on the musical map. I love Fats, and I remember one day when he was late for rehearsal. I had to drive over to his hotel to pick him up. It was 11 A.M., and he had just woken up. He was wearing nothing but underwear, brushing his teeth, and drinking a can of beer. I told him I'd buy him some breakfast, but he kept drinking his beer and said he couldn't eat on an empty stomach.

One of the groups I was proud to have on the show was Buddy Holly & the Crickets. They made their network television debut on *Bandstand* on August 26, 1957, singing a song that would be number one a month later, "That'll Be the Day." Buddy was extremely shy and very difficult to interview. One thing I will never forget is when he said that the only thing he didn't like about his work was flying. Those words rang in my mind when Holly was killed in a plane crash on February 3, 1959, along with two other people I had worked with, the Big Bopper and Ritchie Valens.

If the Academy of Television Arts and Sciences ever asks me for highlights from the fifties that represent *American Bandstand* at its best, I would have to start by selecting a clip of Jackie Wilson. He was called Mr. Excitement, and with good reason. Wilson was one of the most dynamic performers I've ever seen, and he was a strong influence on Elvis Presley, and later on, Michael Jackson and Prince, as well as many other artists. He had been a Golden Gloves boxer and was a fantastic dancer. Jackie made his *Bandstand* debut on October 4, 1957, singing his very first single, "Reet Petite," co-written by Berry Gordy, who later started Motown Records. Jackie Wilson is gone, but his work stands up to this day.

Then I would choose a clip of Bill Haley & His Comets. Haley was far from a teen idol—he had just celebrated his thirtieth birthday three days before "Rock Around the Clock" went to number one, and his receding hairline and portly build made him look much older. However, Haley was as responsible as anyone for bringing rock 'n' roll to mass audiences. It was a thrilling moment in 1955 when in theaters across the land the curtain went up, and *The Blackboard Jungle* began with Haley singing, "One, two, three

moving in

In the late 1940s, as returning GIs were signing on the dotted line to buy their piece of the American Dream—their first homes—no one imagined that suburbia would become an American lifestyle. Thousands of families moved their precious belongings into newly built identical homes in Levittown, New York, (opposite) in 1951 to give their kids fresh air and a safe place to grow up. It wasn't until the sixties, when the charm of suburbia had worn off, that the music industry came up with a hit song about the suburban experience. Pete Seeger's "Little Boxes" (1961) described life in the suburbs, but it wasn't about the Garden of Eden. Suburbia was a land of conformity where everyone lived in the same "ticky, tacky house on a ticky, tacky street." Teens had a hard time finding their own place in the suburban experience. Bandstand provided a gang of friends and a party every day in their own living rooms.

o'clock, four o'clock, rock!" I'd also choose a performance by Fats Domino. The Fat Man made his first *Bandstand* appearance on March 6, 1959, and did a rousing performance of "When the Saints Go Marching In." It's a classic. We had a lot of the other founding fathers of rock 'n' roll on the show in the fifties, like Chuck Berry and Little Richard, but the other clip I would include in a highlights package would be a performance by Frankie Avalon. As the decade evolved, rock music did, too. It moved from the rebelliousness of Elvis Presley to a smoother sound, personified by teen idols like Avalon. Even when he sang his first hit, "DeDe Dinah," through his nose, the girls watching from the bleachers couldn't stop screaming. If you want to know if someone is going to be a big star, watch the audience respond to them. There was no question, based on how the teenagers responded to Frankie, he was going to be very popular.

As the fifties drew to a close, *American Bandstand* was a huge success, drawing millions of viewers every day. My life felt abundant beyond any of my dreams. I was famous, too, swept up in the rock 'n' roll phenomenon as one of the most highly visible people in the nation, thanks to a daily TV series. Things couldn't have been better. But, I wouldn't have been so certain of that if I could have seen just a few weeks into the future.

American Bandstand was the first national TV show to feature teens off the street. Carmen MonteCarlo and Charlie Zamil (below) were two high school students who danced on the show five times a week. Bandstand dancers were local Philadelphia kids fourteen to eighteen years old, mostly from two high schools, West Catholic and South Philadelphia, who came to dance and to be seen dancing every afternoon from 2:30 to 5:00 P.M. It was after-school fun, a way for the teenagers to express who they were. And, for a nationwide teen population with nine billion dollars to spend in allowance money, Bandstand was the showcase for the latest records, the hippest fashions, and the newest products. The teens watching at home finally had a show that they felt a part of, learned from, and measured themselves against. Vera Badamo, who grew up in Brooklyn in the fifties, remembers how "wonderful it was to come home every day and tune in Bandstand and see Italian kids, just like me. You never saw them on regular TV. And, to see some of them wearing Catholic school uniforms was extraordinary. I realized the kids in Philly were just like the kids in Brooklyn."

Lou DeSera (above), a teen who appeared on American Bandstand several times a week, was loved for his slicked-back, pumped-up pompadour. In the late fifties, Philadelphia boys were split on how to wear their hair. South Philadelphians styled it high and shiny; North Philadelphians, inspired by TV's Peter Gunn, wore their hair short and close to their heads, combed to the side. For guys, tweed jackets, button-down shirts, and thin patterned ties were the uniform.

When American Bandstand *went national on August 5, 1957, it had lined up affiliates on a small network of sixty-seven stations. A map of the United States (left) in the studio was dotted with affiliate flags. But by the end of the first year, the show was seen in 4,000,000 homes and local stations were clamoring to come aboard. American Bandstand was as much a neighborhood dance as it was a national television show. Dancing was an integral part of life in Philadelphia, the city that starts the New Year dancing up Broad Street in the centuries-old Mummers' Parade. The rest of the year there were dances everywhere, from St. Alice's School where more than 2,000 teens gathered on Friday and Sunday nights to the very small VFW dances in Southwest Philadelphia where twenty people might show up.*

top teen tv shows

Adventures of Ozzie and Harriet (1952–66)
Bachelor Father (1957–62)
The Brady Bunch (1969–74)
Charlie's Angels (1976–81)
The Danny Thomas Show (1953–71)
The Donna Reed Show (1958–66)
Dr. Kildare (1961–66)
Facts of Life (1979–88)
Fame (1982–83)
Family Ties (1982–89)
Father Knows Best (1954–63)
The Flying Nun (1967–70)
Good Times (1974–79)
Happy Days (1974–84)
Leave It to Beaver (1957–63)
Many Loves of Dobie Gillis (1957–63)
Married with Children (1987–)
The Mod Squad (1968–73)
The Monkees (1966–68)
My Three Sons (1960–72)
Our Miss Brooks (1952–56)
The Partridge Family (1970–74)
The Patty Duke Show (1963–66)
Peyton Place (1964–69)
Room 222 (1969–74)
Route 66 (1960–64)
77 Sunset Strip (1958–64)
That Girl (1966–71)
The Twilight Zone (1959–65)
The Waltons (1972–81)
What's Happening!! (1976–79)

TELEPROMPTER

early deejays

Hoss Allen
Bob Barry
Dick Biondi
Jack Carney
Frankie "The Love Man" Crocker
"Big Daddy" Tom Donahue
Dr. Jive
Fat Daddy
Arnie "Woo Woo" Ginsburg
Hunter Hancock
Jocko Henderson
Casey "At the Mike" Kasem
Herb Kent "the Cool Gent"
Russ "Weird Beard" Knight
Uncle Mike McKuen
Cousin Bruce Morrow
Murray the K
Joe Niagara
Jean Nobles
Dewey Phillips
Bill Randle
Dusty Rhodes
Barry Richards
  ("The Boss with the Hot Sauce")
John Richbough
Danny Schecter
Zenas Sears
Robin Seymour
Dusty Street
Wolfman Jack
Georgie Woods

Dick Clark's world was records—playing them, producing them, promoting them, and even pressing them. During the fifties, both the 45 RPM and rock 'n' roll had a meteoric rise that would change popular music forever. Until then, recorded music was primarily heard on the heavy, awkward, and breakable 78 RPMs. The 45 made the 78 obsolete; it was light, small, and practically indestructible. And because it was cheaper to manufacture, it gave small independent record companies a fighting chance in the industry. Rock 'n' roll was born with the 45 RPM. Teens could easily carry the cheap, seven-inch disks to parties. In 1957, 45s cost sixty-nine cents in Philadelphia, and in many places, if you bought six, you got one free. Because Dick moved with the times, by the end of the decade he owned or had interest in thirty-three companies associated with the record business.

Dancing in the 1950s was an extension of pre-war dances. Couples touched; boys led and girls followed. But within the prescribed formats, individuality reigned. Pat Molittieri (above) demonstrates her expertise in the Jitterbug, the most popular dance on early Bandstand shows. Each dancer had his or her particular style of Jitterbugging, but Pat's was the most unique—she bounced. One of the most popular teens on the show, she had her own advice columns in several teen magazines.

▲ The premise of Arthur and Kathryn Murray's popular fifties TV show, *Arthur Murray's Dance Party*, was that they could teach anyone "dancing in a hurry." By the time the Murrays (above) came to television in 1950, they had opened dance studios throughout the country. Coincidentally, they had also been Dick Clark's neighbors in Mount Vernon, New York. Clark attributed his skills at the Fox Trot to their teaching methods. For years the couple taught TV viewers how to Rumba and Waltz, and sometimes even to Swing, but when Americans began Strolling and Twisting in the late fifties the show had run its course; it vanished from television in 1960.

XEROX

31

When the kids on American Bandstand were not Strolling, or Twisting, or Cha-lypsoing, they were usually Jitterbugging. The Jitterbug was a Philadelphia staple, and there were as many variations as there were Philly neighborhoods. The dance began in the 1920s in the bars of Harlem and took steps from the Shag and the Charleston. Although dancers did wild improvisational solos as part of the Jitterbug, it was essentially a partner dance. In 1927, the solos gave rise to a new variation, the Lindy Hop, named after Charles Lindbergh who had just made his historic solo flight across the Atlantic. The Jitterbug gained wide popularity in the thirties when Swing was at its peak. During World War II, U.S. soldiers took the dance around the world, and it was recognized as quintessentially American.

Few things are as much fun for teenagers as dancing. It's a chance to show off and to be noticed. For the teens on American Bandstand like Barbara Marcen (above), it was a chance to be seen by millions. The dancers, especially the regulars, were always jostling for a spot in front. "We were brats about it," remembers Arlene Sullivan. "We wanted to strut our stuff in front of America," says Bunny Gibson. "But," says Carole Scaldeferri, "Dick didn't want us hogging the camera." "He used the studio mike to get us away from the front. You'd be dancing, and all of a sudden you'd hear Dick's voice telling you to drop back to the rear," says Kenny Rossi. Myrna Horowitz says, "Dick wanted to give everybody a chance. I didn't like dropping back, but I understood it."

Postwar teens were a rebellious lot, and many adults believed their rebellion was not only encouraged by rock 'n' roll, but caused by it. Unlike the popular music that came before it, rock music was loud and raucous, and many parents believed it made kids unruly and destructive. The public riots that often broke out at local rock 'n' roll shows and teen movies were their evidence. After blocking traffic to get into Brooklyn's Paramount Theater in 1957, teens tossing off theater etiquette jumped up and danced in the aisles to a rock 'n' roll beat (below right).

▲ Arlene Sullivan and Kenny Rossi (above, at right) danced together on American Bandstand for a little more than a year. At the height of their popularity, they received as many as 500 letters a day. Arlene, whose mother was a devoted fan, claims she danced on the show "to get my mother's attention." Within three months, Arlene was a regular appearing five days a week. "I was always surprised," she says, "that people wanted my autograph. I danced on a TV show; nothing I did was different than what kids were doing in their own basements. But maybe that's why we were so popular. We were them, and they were us."

BOP

Justine Carelli (above) was American Bandstand's girl next door. Always conservatively dressed and neatly coiffed, Justine was the girl every mother wanted to see her son marry. She first danced on the show when she was only twelve, two years younger than the rules allowed, thanks to her sister's birth certificate and make-up. Justine was an instant hit; in a few weeks she was a regular. When Justine met Bob Clayton and they started dancing and dating, her popularity soared—the two personified the innocent lyrics of the songs they danced to.

▲ Considering the kind of rock 'n' roll being played when she came on the music scene, Connie Francis (above) was right when she said, "A girl can't sing rock 'n' roll too well. It's basically too savage." Girl singers of the fifties were not unlike their counterparts in the forties, neatly dressed, well-coiffed, and ladylike. Born Concetta Franconero in Newark, New Jersey, Francis won first place playing the accordion and singing on Arthur Godfrey's Talent Scouts when she was twelve. She recorded a new version of "Who's Sorry Now" (1957). The record sat at the bottom of the charts for months until Dick Clark played it on American Bandstand the following year. Francis became an instant star, and the record shot up the charts to number four. Francis's international success and hit albums in six languages, put her in a category all her own. Between 1958 and 1963, she had twenty-five records in the top one hundred, including "Stupid Cupid" (1958), "Lipstick on Your Collar" (1959), and "Where the Boys Are" (1961).

▶ Danny and the Juniors (right), who appeared on American Bandstand's anniversary show in 1958, was a group of four teen-aged boys from Philadelphia whose members went to John Bartram High School with some of the show's regulars. Danny (Rapp) and the Juvenairs sang on street corners until Artie Singer of Singular Records happened to hear one of their songs, "Do the Bop." He took it to Dick Clark who, realizing the Bop was on its way out as a dance craze, suggested they change the lyrics. The song got a new title, "At the Hop" (1957), which overnight became a number one hit. The group's "Rock and Roll Is Here to Stay" (1958) became a teen anthem later the same year.

SPLIT LEVEL

The Platters (above) got congratulations on their first hit "Only You" (1955) from Bandstand producer, Tony Mammarella. That same year their "The Great Pretender" hit number one, making the song the first R & B ballad to cross over onto the pop charts. With pop hits like "My Prayer" (1956), "Smoke Gets in Your Eyes" (1958), and "Harbor Lights" (1960) the group broke the color barrier and set the standard for harmony and style for all vocal groups that followed.

By the time Don and Phil Everly (right) recorded their first record for Cadence in 1957, they had already been featured stars of their parents' radio show where they worked out the intimate harmonies that would mark their unique sound and make them the most influential duo in rock 'n' roll history. Their song "Bye Bye Love" (1957), had been turned down by thirty other artists, but it was perfect for their sound. Between 1957 and 1960, the Everly Brothers had a hit every four months including "Wake Up Little Susie" (1957), "All I Have To Do Is Dream" (1958), "Bird Dog" (1958), "('Til) I Kissed You" (1959), "When Will I Be Loved" (1960), and "Let It Be Me" (1960). "Cathy's Clown" (1960) blazed up the charts to become their biggest selling single.

The first record played on the premiere network installment of American Bandstand was Jerry Lee Lewis's call to action, "Whole Lot of Shakin' Going On" (1957). His sharp clothes and animated performances—Lewis (below) was known for kicking the piano stool out from under him, playing the piano standing up, banging out chords, rocking from side to side, and wildly tossing his hair—electrified audiences. The success of "Great Balls of Fire" (1958) sent the dapper singer's career into the stratosphere.

Sam Phillips of Sun Records once lamented that if he "could find a white man who had a Negro sound and the Negro feel," he could make a billion dollars. Phillips probably never made a billion dollars, but he did find the white man, Elvis Aaron Presley. The eighteen-year-old Presley arrived at the Memphis Recording Service in 1953 to record two records for himself. He wasn't happy with the results, but a secretary at the studio was. She noted "good ballad singer" on his tape. Presley's first record for Sam Phillips, "That's All Right" (1954), hit the top of the country charts within ten days of its release. In 1956, his records dominated the national charts. That year Presley had eleven gold records, including "Heartbreak Hotel," "Blue Suede Shoes," "Hound Dog," and "Don't Be Cruel." Presley sold one billion records in his career, had sixty-seven top twenty singles, and thirty-eight top twenty albums. He was the indisputable king of rock 'n' roll.

Little Richard Penniman shot the opening salvo in the rock 'n' roll revolution with the words "awop bop a lu bop, alop bam boom!" What they mean is still anybody's guess, except that they were a cleaned-up version of a song Little Richard sang off-mike during a recording session in 1955. From the outset, Little Richard had spunk and ambition. His outrageous hair-do and piano-pounding style singled him out from the group of black rhythm and blues singers who were moving into the national consciousness. Outspoken and flamboyant, he sent shock waves through the music industry. Thought to be too much for the average record buyer or radio listener, he proved critics wrong, drawing fans that appreciated his style.

COUNT-DOWN

With thirty-five records a day to play, the producers of American Bandstand were constantly searching for new material. Clark met in his office regularly with representatives of the record industry (left) to keep apprised of the latest releases and the newest singers and groups. But in 1959, following the scandalous revelation that Charles Van Doren had been given answers while a contestant on the popular TV quiz show Twenty-One (1956–1958), questions were raised about the honesty of the record industry. Investigators alleged that deejays accepted bribes to play certain songs, otherwise there was no way to explain why many rock 'n' roll songs had become popular. Being the number one deejay in the country, Clark was called to testify at the 1959–60 Congressional hearings on payola. He swore he never took money or gifts, but he was still forced to give up his interests in the record business.

43

rock, rock, rock

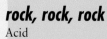

Acid
Blues
Bubblegum
Christian
Corporate
Cowboy
Disco
Funk
Fusion
Glitter Rock
Hard
Heavy Metal
Hillbilly
House
New Wave
Pet
Progressive
Psychedelic
Punk
Reggae-ska
Rockabilly
Soft
Soul
Surf
Techno
Thrash

With a college degree in advertising and an uncanny ability to speak to teenagers, Dick Clark was the perfect pitchman for sponsors whose products—from shampoo to acne medication to watches—were targeted at the adolescent market. In the late fifties, as the teenage market expanded and the number of teenagers jumped from seven million to twelve million, Clark shifted from being a local spokesperson for Barr's, a popular Philadelphia jewelry store, to a national spokesperson doing endorsements for hair tonic, chewing gum, and soda. He helped line up enough sponsors to make American Bandstand one of television's most profitable daytime shows.

One way to spotlight the songs, the dancers, and the dances on American Bandstand was to hold dance contests (below). Kids in the studio loved them, and the viewers did, too. The rules were simple. Contestants had to sign up to get a number, then once a week they pinned the numbers on their backs, much as they did in the marathon dances of the thirties. During the contests, viewers cast ballots for their favorite dancers. Each contest lasted three or four weeks, after which the winners were announced on air. Several of the winners confessed that the voting was done more on popularity than merit. Still, they took their prizes, which ranged from portable TVs to jukeboxes.

▲ Dick Clark inherited the original set for American Bandstand (above) from Bob Horn's Bandstand, the show Clark took over in 1956. The painted background was of a record shop of the late forties or early fifties, when records were still big, clunky 78 RPMs. Clark's high podium, like a bandstand, set him apart from the dancers. The podium was donated in 1981 to the Smithsonian Institution.

LITTERBUG

"Joanne, seventeen, South Philly," "Mark J., fourteen, Bartram," "Scott, fifteen, North Catholic." Roll Call (above) was a regular feature on American Bandstand and was how the viewers at home got to know the kids on the show. When the show was only broadcast locally, the kids gave the names of their schools, as well as their names and ages. When the show went national in 1957, they gave their names, ages, and their hometowns.

BEATNIK

Kids watching Bandstand at home were looking for any clues that signaled romance between the kids on the show—who danced with whom, how closely they danced, and how often they slow danced together. In the innocent fifties, euphemisms for touching and sex abounded in American culture, especially on television. Harmless games—where kids came into more intimate contact with each other—spiced up the Bandstand programs. In this awkward moment, teens cooperate to "eat" up the string attached to a marshmallow (left). Of course, if both partners succeeded, they came as close to kissing each other as was possible on a show that morally towed the line.

Johnny Mathis signs autographs at the autograph table during his October 15, 1957, debut on American Bandstand (right). For teens who grew up in the fifties, Mathis was the unchallenged make-out king, whose silky smooth voice easily filled a darkened room. When Mathis released two singles in 1957, "Wonderful! Wonderful!" and "It's Not for Me to Say," teenagers had their Frank Sinatra. The following year, he had seven hits, including the classic "Chances Are." His album, Johnny's Greatest Hits (1958), the first of the greatest hits albums, remained on the charts for a record 490 weeks. Only Pink Floyd's Dark Side of the Moon (1979) surpassed it.

"It's got a great beat and you can dance to it." Those immortal words came to represent one of the most popular features of American Bandstand, Record Review. The formula was simple: three kids listened to three records, and rated them between thirty-five and ninety-eight. A fourth teen calculated the average, often with the help of Dick Clark (left). The kids were usually right in their judgments, picking scores of songs that became top ten winners, demonstrating once again how their opinions counted.

For millions of American teens who could not get to Philadelphia to meet their favorite regulars in the American Bandstand studio, the next best thing was voting for them in one of the show's many dance contests. The contests were a regular feature, giving viewers a chance to see their favorite couples and the newest dances. Tens of thousands of fans sent their ballots to American Bandstand, PO Box 6, Philadelphia 5, Pa. In a normal week, the show received about 45,000 letters. During the contests, 150,000 ballots and letters came in, prompting Clark to joke that all the mail bags in Philadelphia were being used to carry mail to the show.

AMERICAN BANDSTAND - P.O. BO

PONY DANCE CONTEST WIN

- 1st. PRIZE - No.3 {FRANI G
{MIKE B

- 2nd. PRIZE - No.4 {JOYCE
{NORMA

- 3rd. PRIZE - No.9 {CARMEN
{FRANN

CHEVALIER

DO-IT-YOURSELF

As audiences for Bandstand grew, so did the stakes for dance contest winners, who took home prizes that ranged from record albums to brand new automobiles. (Left to right) Frani Giordano and Mike Balara, Joyce Schaeffer and Norman Kerr, and Carmen Jimenez and Frank Vacca eye the first-prize in the Pony contest, the shiny new convertible that went to Frani and Mike.

With five shows a week, fifty-two weeks a year, the producers of American Bandstand had to come up with features to keep the show fresh, interesting, and fun. One way was to celebrate Christmas, New Year's, and Halloween. The Halloween shows were the most amusing since they incorporated games, masks, and special guest stars like the ghoulish Zacherle performing the novelty hit, "Dinner with Drac Part I" (1958). One of the most popular games was musical chairs, where the masked teens rushed to find a seat when the music stopped, and others ended up on the studio floor. The thin line between childish and teenage behavior sometimes evaporated with party games that were silly but made for good fun and, more importantly, better TV.

SCI-FI

> Sitting in bleachers is one of the most common things a teen does—at football games, track meets, dances, shows, and sometimes even at church. They do it at school, in choir, and at graduation. Using bleachers on American Bandstand made the set feel familiar. But as regular Arlene Sullivan remembers, "They were hard and very uncomfortable." (First row, fourth and fifth girls) Carmen and Ivette Jimenez watched as Dick interviewed one of his daily guests.

▼ One of the most popular dances created by the Bandstand crowd was the Cha-lypso, a combination of two popular fifties dances, the Cha-cha and the Calypso. The simple dance could be done to songs as different as The Shirelles' "Will You Love Me Tomorrow"(1957) and Gene Pitney's "Every Breath I Take" (1958). When the Cha-lypso became popular, several songs were written specifically for it; the most successful was Billy and Lillie's "La Dee Dah" (1957). Two dancers (below) demonstrated the steps to Dick Clark.

stylish 'dos

girls
Artichoke
B-52
Beehive
Disco wedge
Dorothy Hamill
Farrah Fawcett
Flip
French twist
Page boy
Pixie
Sassoon cut
Shag

boys
Afro
Beatle
Butch
Collegiate
Crew cut
D.A.
Dry look
Flat top
Lounge Lizard
Mohawk
Pompadour
Punk
Razor cut
Sidewalls
Square back
Tony Manero
Uneasy Rider
Wet look

By the end of the decade, the suggestive, dynamic music that characterized the restless years of the fifties gave way to romantic tuneful songs about teenage love. The mastermind behind this change was Don Kirschner, a songwriter, who with a partner, Al Nevins, formed Aldon Music. In 1958, a young Neil Sedaka (above) and his high school friend Howie Greenfield walked into Kirschner's office and played six songs for Kirschner: "Stupid Cupid," "The Diary," and "Calendar Girl" among them. Connie Francis was tapped to record "Stupid Cupid" (1958), but after the song hit with Francis, Sedaka began recording his own tunes. "The Diary" (1959) was his first hit, followed by "Happy Birthday Sweet Sixteen" (1961), "Breaking Up is Hard to Do" (1962), and "Oh, Carol" (1959) written about his friend who became the successful songwriter and singer, Carole King.

Dick Clark's unique talent was taking the music that America was afraid of—rock 'n' roll—and broadcasting it for teens who loved it while introducing it to the adults who hated it. Well-dressed and well-behaved, Clark and the kids on American Bandstand (above) were instrumental in popularizing a new kind of music that was under attack by everyone from Frank Sinatra, "the most brutal, ugly, desperate, vicious form of expression it has been my misfortune to hear;" to Sammy Davis Jr., "If rock 'n' roll is here to stay, I might commit suicide;" to author Vance Packard, "Rock music might be best summed up as monotony tinged with hysteria;" to Tip O'Neill, then Speaker of the House, who said in 1960, "Rock and roll is a type of sensuous music unfit for impressionable minds."

If imitation is the greatest form of flattery, American Bandstand is one of the most flattered shows in television history. The format for the show required only four things: a deejay, a podium, records, and kids. Adults copied the format for local dances, civic functions, and, sometimes, for television shows. But for school kids, following the format was a way to re-create the Bandstand scene. In the version of American Bandstand acted out at this junior high school, the kids followed a script (below) and even had a top ten list that reflected the most popular songs around Halloween 1958.

WEATHER MAP OF THE UNITED STATES

LAKESIDE SCHOOL

DETROIT

AMERICAN BANDSTAND

Script

We recorded your theme song on tape and played it as the curtains opened—— we were dancing.

DICK CLARK - Hi!!! Welcome to American Bandstand. Let's line up for "The Stroll" by the Diamonds.

We had two groups doing the stroll.

DICK CLARK - Head for the hills. Here's Jerry Lee Lewis singing the song that made him famous, "Great Balls of Fire".

Kids scream and yell...... girls do little step done on Bandstand and squeal.

"Our" Jerry Lee Lewis pantomined to the record.

Kids scream for more at the end of the song.

DICK CLARK - Crazy!!!!! What are your future plans?

JERRY LEE - I'm making an album on the "Sun" label.

DICK CLARK - Fine! Your next stop is the Autograph Table. Okay?

JERRY LEE -- Fine!

Kids run for autographs

DICK CLARK -- Now where are our three couples for the "Spotlight Dance"?

The three couples come to the center of the stage.

DICK CLARK - Good. Your names and ages, please.

They give their names and ages.

DICK CLARK - FINE. It's a slow one, so you may take the whole floor. Here's Pat Boone with "It's Too Soon to Know".

Couples dance.

DICK CLARK - Well, it's just about time to go. Here's "Rock and Roll is Here to Stay" by Danny and the Juniors.

We dance to record.

DICK CLARK - Here's our Theme Song. What is it?

KIDS - "Bandstand Boogie"!!!!!!!!!

DICK CLARK - Right.

Curtains close while we danc to the music recorded from your show....

BARBIE

The transistor radio (left), invented by Texas Instruments in 1954, not only changed what teens listened to, it made rock 'n' roll ubiquitous. Until then, most people heard music on 78 RPM records, large console radios, or in person at concerts. The small, portable radio allowed teens to listen to music away from their parents—anytime, anywhere. They could stick a radio in their pockets and listen to their favorite tunes in school, walking down the street, or in bed when they were supposed to be asleep. The popularity of the radios established the careers of the greatest advocates for rock 'n' roll, the deejays, who in city after city defied the powers that be and played the new, provocative music.

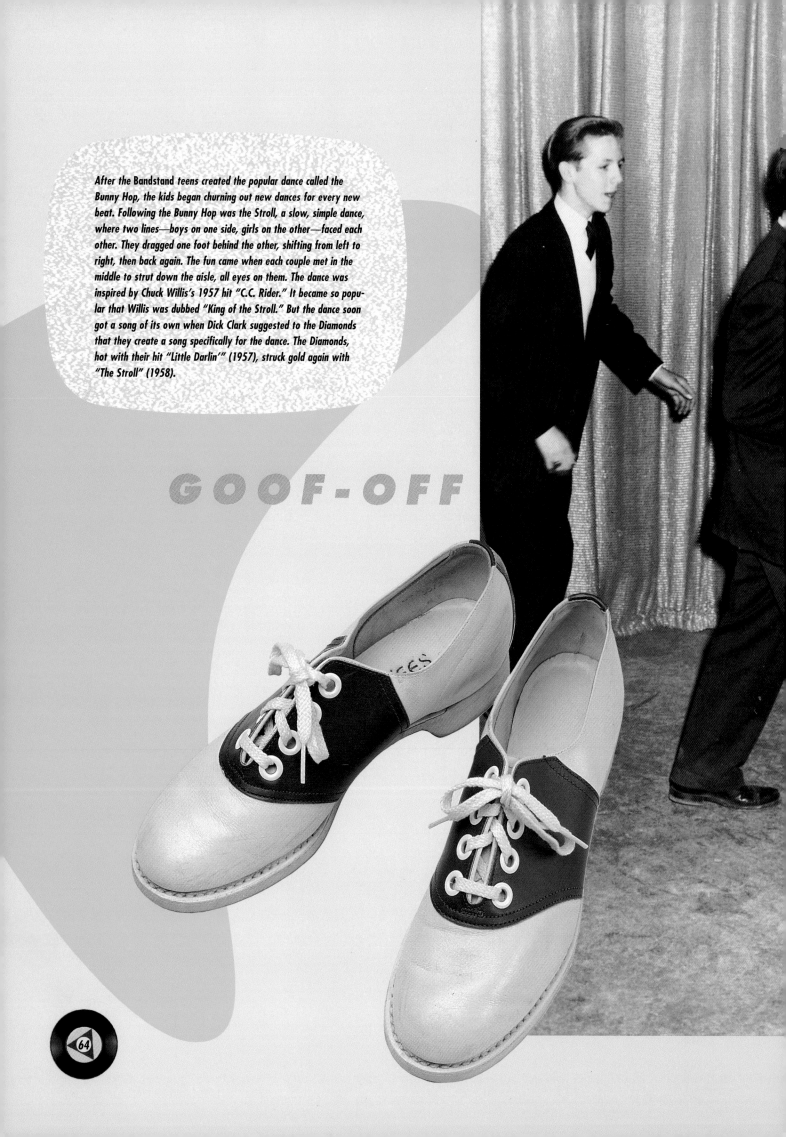

After the Bandstand teens created the popular dance called the Bunny Hop, the kids began churning out new dances for every new beat. Following the Bunny Hop was the Stroll, a slow, simple dance, where two lines—boys on one side, girls on the other—faced each other. They dragged one foot behind the other, shifting from left to right, then back again. The fun came when each couple met in the middle to strut down the aisle, all eyes on them. The dance was inspired by Chuck Willis's 1957 hit "C.C. Rider." It became so popular that Willis was dubbed "King of the Stroll." But the dance soon got a song of its own when Dick Clark suggested to the Diamonds that they create a song specifically for the dance. The Diamonds, hot with their hit "Little Darlin'" (1957), struck gold again with "The Stroll" (1958).

GOOF-OFF

In the 1950s and '60s the last dance at record hops was usually a slow dance. Whether it was the Flamingos crooning "Lovers Never Say Goodbye" (1959) or Jesse Belvin lamenting "Good Night My Love" (1956), teenagers grabbed their special partners and slowly circled the dance floor. Slow dancing was intimate, or as Dick Clark characterized it, "getting sexually aroused with no payoff." Despite the lights and cameras and the fact that six million people were watching, the kids on American Bandstand managed to enter that dreamy world of slow dancing.

One of the hazards of dancing on American Bandstand was the miles of thick, black cable that wove itself around the dance floor, for the huge TV cameras dominated the floor. A white line separated the cameras from the dancers, but the line was constantly violated as the camera searched for better pictures of the dancing kids. Often teens had to stop dancing to step over the cable, an awkwardness rarely seen by viewers at home.

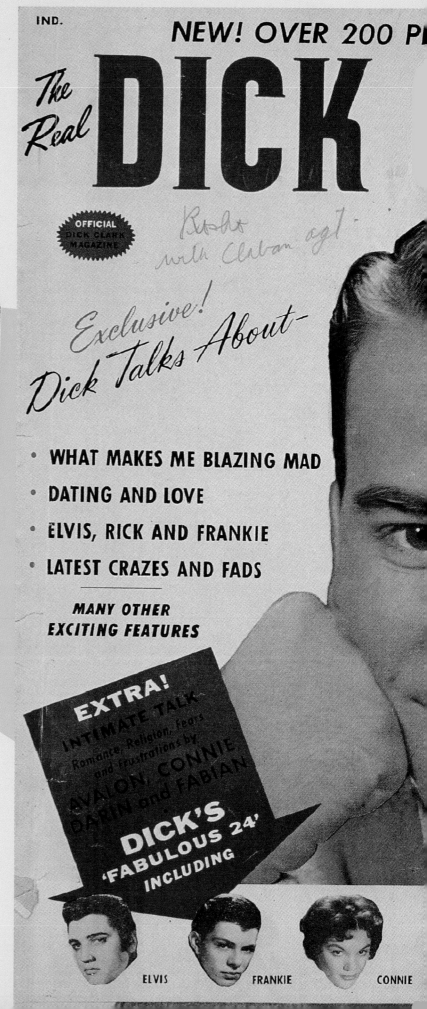

Youthful, non-threatening, and telegenic, Dick Clark was a TV personality, movie star, radio host, and author whose trusted daily presence in American homes brought him celebrity. During *American Bandstand's* heyday, his face was on the TV screen every weekday afternoon, every Saturday night, and for a short time, on Monday nights. In magazine articles, books, and on radio shows, Clark comfortably discussed everything a teenager might worry or wonder about, from music to dating etiquette.

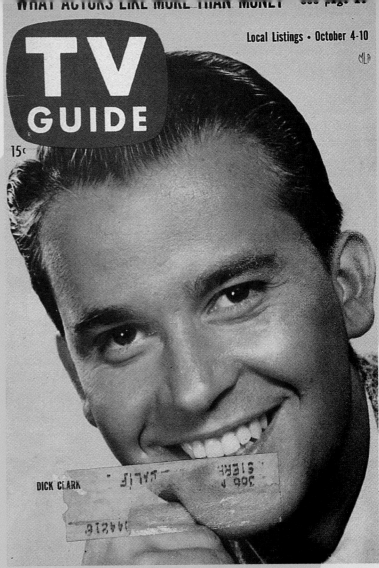

TV GUIDE

15¢

DICK CLARK

DS AND STORIES

LARK

No. 1
35¢

RICKY   PAT   BOBBY

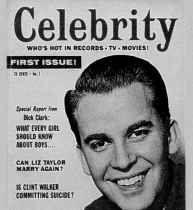

Celebrity

WHO'S HOT IN RECORDS · TV · MOVIES!

FIRST ISSUE!

25 CENTS · No. 1

Special Report from
Dick Clark:
WHAT EVERY GIRL
SHOULD KNOW
ABOUT BOYS...

CAN LIZ TAYLOR
MARRY AGAIN?

IS CLINT WALKER
COMMITTING SUICIDE?

ELVIS PROVES
HIMSELF!
A Book-Length Bonus!

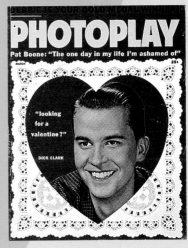

PHOTOPLAY

Pat Boone: "The one day in my life I'm ashamed of"

MARCH   25¢

"looking
for a
valentine?"

DICK CLARK

69

Fabian was not a singer when he was singled out for stardom. But Fabian (born Fabiano Forte) studied hard, learning to sing, walk, talk, and act. He spent time at concerts watching other performers, and it paid off. In 1959, he had three hits, "Turn Me Loose," "Tiger," and "Hound Dog Man." Like Avalon, Fabian left Philly for Hollywood. By the end of the sixties, he had made more than a dozen films.

Bobby Rydell was born Robert Ridarellii, and was the third of Philly's big teen idols. When stardom came for him, he was ready. Recording for Cameo Records, he hit big in 1959 with "Kissin' Time." Over the next four years, Rydell had nineteen top twenty hits including the million seller "Volare" (1960), a cover version of Domenico Modugno's 1958 hit, "Nel Blu Di Pinto Di Blu." Like his friends Fabian and Frankie Avalon, Rydell went to Hollywood. Much of the three teen idols's success was because they all lived close to the American Bandstand studio. At a moment's notice—when the studio telephoned—they could replace a guest who hadn't shown up. Each had a good rapport with Dick Clark, who visited them in their South Philadelphia homes. The surprise was that, despite their fame and fortune, they lived modestly like many of the kids who watched the show.

After years of glamorous teen rebels, making teen idols safe was one of the ideas behind the celebrity machine that Chancellor Records created in the late fifties. Two of the boys chosen—Frankie Avalon (below) and Fabian—were white, Italian, likable, easy-going teens from the same South Philadelphia neighborhood. Avalon was Chancellor's first success. His initial releases in 1957, "Cupid" and "Teacher's Pet," were bombs. His third release, "DeDe Dinah" (1958), an innocuous ditty that even Avalon said he had no feel for, sold a million copies, and was the first of his six top ten hits. Avalon soon left Philadelphia for Hollywood and found movie stardom on the blankets of several beach movies with his partner, Annette Funicello.

October 27, 1959, was "Brenda Lee Day" on American Bandstand
(below). The 4'11" dynamo had been performing since she was a tod-
dler, and by the age of six had her own fifteen-minute television show.
By twelve, she had several regional country hit songs, including
"Dynamite" (1957), the song that gave her her nickname, "Little Miss
Dynamite." In 1958, she recorded one of the best rock 'n' roll
Christmas songs ever, "Rockin' Around the Christmas Tree," which for
some reason was not released until 1960, when it went to the top of
the charts. "I'm Sorry," "Sweet Nothin's," and "I Want to Be Wanted"
were in the top ten the next year. In 1962, when she was only eighteen, she made "Break It to Me Gently," a ballad whose emotional
message would have been difficult for a singer twice her age.

BRENDA LEE DAY

rebel flics

Blackboard Jungle (1955)
Drag Strip Girl (1957)
Eighteen and Anxious (1957)
The Explosive Generation (1961)
High School Confidential (1958)
Hot Rod Alley (1956)
Hot Rod Gang (1958)
Hot Rod Girl (1956)
Platinum High School (1960)
Rebel Without a Cause (1955)
Reform School Girl (1957)
Rock All Night (1957)
Wild for Kicks (1962)
The Wild One (1954)

A GIRL DELINQUENT ...A JET PROPELLED GANG... OUT FOR FAST KICKS!

JUVENILE JUNGLE

in NATURAMA

STARRING

COREY ALLEN · REBECCA WELLES
RICHARD BAKALYAN
ANNE WHITFIELD · JOE DI REDA

By the mid-fifties, America's post war optimism was beginning to show signs of strain. No where was it more apparent than in the nation's youth. Overnight, American teens became a potent economic and cultural force. For the first time in history, they had time to kill and money to burn, and they rejected almost everything their parents stood for. No wonder their first screen idol was the rebellious James Dean. Movies about tough misunderstood kids who didn't respect society's conventions were cranked out by Hollywood. Double-bill features, like *Juvenile Jungle (1955)* (left), attracted crowds that often erupted into violence. In Philadelphia, a mother whose son had been injured during a screening of Rock Rock Rock (1955) sued the Stanley Warner Theater for $40,000 in damages, claiming her son was beaten and stomped during the showing of the film. The jury was sympathetic, and she won her case.

When anyone remembers Bandstand or American Bandstand they generally think of two things: Dick Clark and the regulars who appeared on the show more than two or three times a week. The regulars, pictured here off-screen, were not actors or professional dancers, but ordinary high school students. The concept of the regular took off when a Bandstand dancer, Tom DeNoble, appeared at a local dance and more than a thousand kids showed up to see him. No one expected so many people, and it was immediately clear to producers that regulars drew a large viewing audience, as well as a dependable studio audience. Becoming a regular was a lot easier than most viewers imagined. If viewers knew your name and wrote to you, you could get a membership card. Bunny Gibson remembers getting mail the second week she was on the show and becoming a regular the third. As a regular you didn't have to wait in line, and, at least in the early days, you could get in to the show every day. As the number of regulars increased, the number of days they appeared decreased. Ed Kelly says he was allowed on the show only on certain days of the week. There were about sixty regulars in the fifties, and many viewers could name them all. For teen viewers, especially outside Philadelphia, the regulars were role models. Girls copied hair-dos and make-up; boys copied dance steps and clothing styles. By the time the show moved to Los Angeles in 1964, where multiple episodes were taped in one day, the regulars were less important to the dynamic of the show.

ARLENE
ANSWERS HER MAIL

Have you written a letter to ARLENE? Well, look here — maybe there's an answer waiting for YOU!

Since I invited you all to drop me a line in care of 16, I have received so many, many letters that I know I'll never be able to sit down and personally answer them all. So I have decided to send each of you who write to me an autographed picture post-card of myself — and to use the pages of 16 from time to time to answer at least some of my mail.

I am going to try and select letters that represent the bulk of my mail, and to answer as many questions and give out as much information as I can.

● *Dear Arlene:*
I watch Bandstand and wanted to ask you a few questions. Tell me about Carmen, Frani, Carole, Barbara, Bunny and Arlene Di Pietro. Are they nice and a lot of fun? How old are you? I would like to meet a star. Have you ever dated a star? How did you meet him? May I please have a picture of you?
Jerri McCullom
Brownstown, Ill.

Dear Jerri:
Carmen, Fran, Barb and all the kids are nice and just wonderful people to know. The newsletter in 16 will keep you right up-to-date on them. I am 18 years old. I guess we all would like to meet stars and to date them, too. I have met Bobby Rydell, Frankie Avalon, Fabian and many others, but I have never dated a star. I am sending you a postcard picture of me.

● *Dear Arlene:*
I was wondering if I could start a fan club for you? I wish you luck in your writing career.
Lydia Cruz
Avondale. Ariz.

Dear Lydia:
Thank you for your kind thoughts. Please write to

Janice and Janet, 569 Duran99 Drive, Toledo 9, Ohio, regarding joining my club or starting one. Enclose a self-addressed, stamped envelope.

● *Dear Arlene:*
Are you still dating Kenny? I would like to have a picture of you and Kenny. Who are your best friends? Who are your favorite singers? Please send me a picture of the Beltrante Sisters also.
Irene Garcia
Oxnard, Calif.

Dear Irene:
Kenny and I are not going steady. We never really did. We still see each other and are the best of friends and always will be. Who knows what the future holds — we're both so young. I am putting one of my favorite pictures of Ken and myself on these pages. My best friends include Carole Gibson, Frani Giordano, Barbara Levick and Steve Brandt. My favorite singers are Paul Anka and Annette. I don't have any photos of Mary or Sue, but you could join their fan club and get some. Susan's is Terry George, 1022 McKumman Road, Fayetteville, N. C., and Mary's is Freda Sansone, 6777 Sunray Ave., Cincinnati 30, Ohio. Please enclose a self-addressed, stamped envelope when you write to them.

● *Dear Arlene:*
This may not sound like much of a problem, but it is to me. I like this boy who goes to my church. I don't know his name, but I know where he lives. My problem is — how do I get to know him? He seems to like me because he looks at me and smiles. I'm sort of bashful!
Darlene H.
Waterville, Mich.

I know how you feel, believe me. I think the only thing you can do is smile right back at him. If you ever get the chance to politely say hello, say it by all means. Don't ever go walking by his house or anything like that. It looks bad. Meeting him eventually through your church activities is the best thing to do.

● *Dear Arlene:*
If I moved to Philadelphia and went to Bandstand, would I be considered a regular? How does someone become a regular? Would you send me a picture of all the regulars?
Rachel De Rogatis
Carteret, N. J.

Dear Rachel:
If you were able to attend American Bandstand every day and were a good dancer, undoubtedly you would soon become a regular. We used to have Band-stand Club cards, but I don't know whether they are still in existence or not. Each kid who goes there regularly has a chance of becoming a regular. I couldn't possibly manage to send you a picture of all the regulars. If you want these badly, why not buy 16's *Secret Bandstand Album?* In it you'll find all the national fan clubs and many of the regulars' home addresses.

● *Dear Arlene:*
There is a girl on Bandstand now named Rose, and she looks like you. Do you know her or anything about her? I wrote to American Bandstand but they never did answer.
Charon Penrose
St. Louis 7, Mo.

Dear Charon:
Her name is Rose Aquilla and we do look alike. It happens that she lives down the street from me. This is 5' 1" tall — and I think she goes steady.

● *Dear Arlene:*
Would you please tell me how you set your hair?
Ann Buker
Deerfield. Ill.

Dear Ann:
First, I wash my hair twice (once a shampoo and rinse it thoroughly. hair short now. I roll it backward across the top of my head (with big wants on the sides and back. When fully comb it out and then set it in spray my hair after I have set it:

● *Dear Arlene:*
I have been to American Bands and I have always wanted to meet ulars — especially Barbara Levick. I am afraid to say anything. How meeting one of the regulars? I have and my mother has often told me more important than good looks. C
Philadelphia, Pa.

Dear Frani:
Your mom is so right! Unfortunately, many people put much too much stress on looks and not enough on the inner qualities, which really count. As far as meeting the regulars go, I think you should drift over during the show one day and just speak to them. Barb isn't going there anymore, but Frani and many of the others will be very friendly, I assure you. Why don't you show them this?

● *Dear Arlene:*
Just out of curiosity, I'd like to know if you were in Cleveland on February 23, 1961? I meant to ask you then, but when I turned around you were gone. If it wasn't you, it was your twin sister.
Janice Hraster
Cleveland, Ohio.

Dear Janice:
It was probably me, as I was visiting friends in Cleveland at that time.

Send letters to Arlene Sullivan, c/o 16 Magazine, 745 Fifth Avenue, New York 22, New York.

Arlene and Kenny. It's her favorite photo.

IVETTE & CARMEN
Your favorite siste

Hi there!
This is going to be fun. See that girl over ther Well, she's my sister, Carmen, and I'm going to gi you the scoop on her.

Carmen Mildred Jimenez was born on June 1945. She is five feet two inches tall and has bla hair and dark brown eyes. She's 105 pounds charged-up dynamite. Carmen goes to Jones High and will be going to Kensington this fall. Al bra is her favorite subject.

Carmen, contrary to popu belief, is really sort of stick-in-the-mud. She does particularly want to see the wo and will be content to marry and set down right in Philly-town. Before all t takes place, she would like to be a sec tary for a couple of years.

But I'm making her do a little traveling t summer when we visit friends in Seattle, C fornia, and the mid-west. You see, Carmen a secret yen to meet a cow (honest — she's nev seen one and is dying to) so that's the lure using to get her to make the trip.

Carmen's Hollywood favorites are Robert Tay and Elizabeth Taylor and her favorite TV show *The Untouchables.* (Traitor!) She loves listening LP's — and flips (and I mean, *flips*) for Freddie C non. Runners-up are Elvis and Brenda Lee. She li to fast dance and we often have the regulars over some of same.

Italian food goes over big with my little sis and her biggest meal is breakfast, at which she vours tomato juice, eggs, toast and hot chocolate. S can't boil an egg, though!

Carmen loves collecting stuffed animals and yea to get a real puppy-dog one day. She even talks some of her stuffed toys. They have great conver tions! I always know all of Carmen's secrets becau she talks in her sleep. She loves to chew bubble gu she's lazy, she steals my sweaters, and she has enou energy for a battalion of Marines. But she is a liv doll — and my favorite person in the whole wor
Bye-bye,
Ivet

Write to Carmen in care of Florence O'Dare, 90 Dibble, Northwest, Seattle, Washington. Send a se addressed, stamped envelope.

20

WIN A DATE WITH JOHNNY TILLOTSON

JULY

16

MAGENZINE

35¢

25¢

RYDELL

BALARA

WE'RE INSIDE TOO.

CHUBBY

BRENDA

DUANE

The LONELY LIFE of **DION**

ANNETTE

How to get HIM to like YOU

SEDAKA

ARLENE

AND NEW PIX

ZE PIN-UP

AVALON

MOR

ell on each other

eam splits up long enough
or each to confide
he other's secrets!

REETINGS!

Two can play this game, you know — so here's the
rd on that little girl standing right over there:

Ivette is five feet three inches tall and weighs 113
unds. She has dark brown hair and eyes and goes
Kensington High School. She is in the 11th grade
d English is her favorite subject. Ivette's
bition to become an airline hostess is
ling fast — and her latest yen is to become
"pop" singer. No comment.

Ivette digs casual clothes, especially Capri slacks
th a blouse and cardigan sweater. She likes
aight skirts, and for dress she would pick a sophis-
ated number in beige or baby blue.

Ivette has a desire to travel, and I doubt that she'll
er settle down. If she does, it will probably be in
llywood. She digs Italian and American food, but
n't boil water herself. Ivette's hobby is collecting
ld jewelry and stuffed animals.

Ivette dearly loves the family (so do I!), which
nsists of Mom (Carmen), dad (Oscar), and my
others and sister — (Orlando, 21; Victor, 23; and
dele, 25). Ivette's middle name is Zaida, which is
anish.

Ivette doesn't have a steady and doesn't believe
going steady. She loves to dance fast, particularly
Connie Francis and Jack Scott records.

Acting awards from Ivette go to Rock Hudson and
lizabeth Taylor. Her favorite TV show is *Thriller*.
Traitor!) One of her favorite pastimes is practicing
sinc-ing the latest hits in front of the mirror. She
very hot on *Blue Moon*.

eriously Ivette is my best friend in the whole world.
e confide in one another and never have any serious
guments. But there is one thing I *must* tell you —
at streak in her hair is *not* real!

Love 'n' stuff,

Carmen

Write to Ivette in care of Barbara Brown, 201 Cooper
reet, Manchester, Pa. Send a self-addressed, stamped

By the end of the fifties, America's teens could not get enough
of the American Bandstand regulars, and they religiously bought
copies of any magazine that featured their pictures and stories,
mostly bylined by the girls. Gloria Stavers, founder of 16 Magazine,
saw profit in the teen magazine market. Her monthly articles featured what teens—or teenage girls—were interested in: beauty
secrets, dating without going too far, how to give a successful
party, how to dress, walk, and talk to impress a boy. She ran
columns by Bandstand regulars like Pat Molittieri, who kept read-
ers up to date with gossip about who was dating whom, who was
about to graduate, and where the regulars were appearing each
month. But it turned out that it was Stavers herself who actually
wrote many of the American Bandstand articles.

AUTOMATED

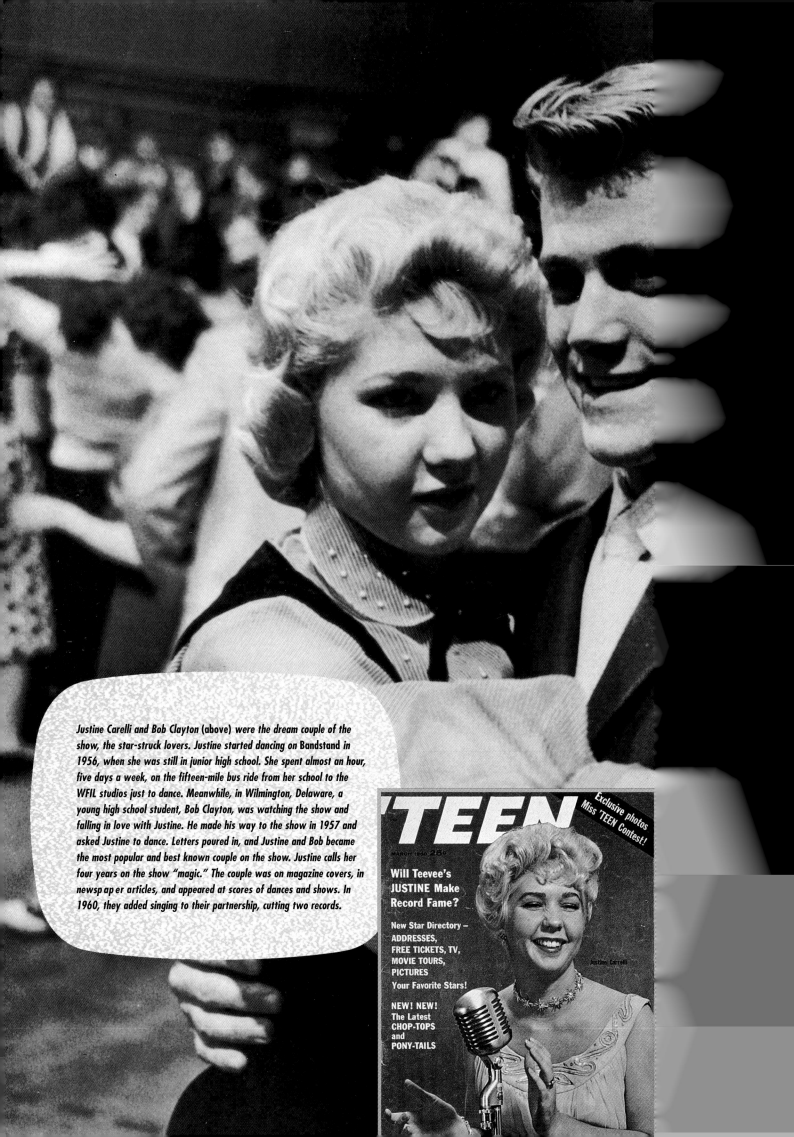

Justine Carelli and Bob Clayton (above) were the dream couple of the show, the star-struck lovers. Justine started dancing on Bandstand in 1956, when she was still in junior high school. She spent almost an hour, five days a week, on the fifteen-mile bus ride from her school to the WFIL studios just to dance. Meanwhile, in Wilmington, Delaware, a young high school student, Bob Clayton, was watching the show and falling in love with Justine. He made his way to the show in 1957 and asked Justine to dance. Letters poured in, and Justine and Bob became the most popular and best known couple on the show. Justine calls her four years on the show "magic." The couple was on magazine covers, in newspaper articles, and appeared at scores of dances and shows. In 1960, they added singing to their partnership, cutting two records.

'TEEN

Exclusive photos Miss 'TEEN Contest!

MARCH 1960 25¢

Will Teevee's
JUSTINE Make
Record Fame?

New Star Directory —
ADDRESSES,
FREE TICKETS, TV,
MOVIE TOURS,
PICTURES
Your Favorite Stars!

NEW! NEW!
The Latest
CHOP-TOPS
and
PONY-TAILS

Justine Carelli

Sincerely
Bob Clayton

The popularity of regulars like Bob Clayton (above) spawned fan clubs, loosely-knit organizations dedicated to honoring the lives and images of favorite dancers. For less than a dollar, fans got a membership card, background information, an autographed picture, and a periodic newsletter, which kept fans abreast of where their favorite regulars would be appearing, what he or she liked to do for fun, and who was dating whom. Dave Frees, who heads the American Bandstand Fan Club, remembers when the president of Carmen Jimenez's fan club went off to college and offered him the club, he jumped at the opportunity. Over the years, he picked up the fan clubs to virtually every regular who appeared on the show during its Philadelphia days. Today he has over one thousand members in the American Bandstand Fan Club.

A DAY AND A HALF IN SPACE

CBS NEWS

FORD RAILROAD CO. · TICKETS

WESTCLOX

CLOCKS

KEEPS AMERICA ON TIM

HARD DAY'S NIGHT

It was a cold, wintry day in Philadelphia when we returned from our New Year's break on Monday, January 4, 1960, to do our first *American Bandstand* of the decade. The WFIL studio seemed warm by comparison, even though we had to hold the temperature down in the low fifties to keep those huge black-and-white cameras working. The kids had dumped their parkas and boots backstage and were dancing away to the number five song in the nation, "Way Down Yonder in New Orleans" by Freddie Cannon. I introduced our guest act of the day, a group of teenagers from New Mexico called the Fireballs. A few years later they would have a number one hit with "Sugar Shack," but today they were performing their current instrumental hit "Bulldog." It was hard to pay attention to their guitar licks. Instead, I found myself looking over the faces of our regulars and wondering if they knew how close we had come a few weeks ago to saying goodbye to *American Bandstand* forever, and that in the next few months they might very well be on the losing side of a cultural war that would bring down this television show, my career, and rock 'n' roll.

Just eight weeks earlier I had been called into the office of Leonard Goldenson, the President of ABC-Paramount. I had great respect for the man and over the years have counted him as a close friend and mentor. But that day, as I sat opposite his desk, there was

the longest voyage
As rock musicians in the late sixties were exploring new frontiers in music, America's astronauts were pushing the boundaries of outer space. On July 20, 1969, millions of people gathered around TV sets in their living rooms, or crowded together beneath giant screens in public places like New York City's Grand Central Terminal (opposite), to watch U.S. astronaut Neil Armstrong fulfill man's centuries-old dream of setting foot on the moon. In 1962, the U.S. put the first communications satellite, Telstar, into orbit. The launch inspired English songwriter Joe Meek's futuristic composition "Telstar" that same year. The Tornadoes recorded the instrumental and the record soared to the number one spot around the world.

only a moment for opening pleasantries before he asked me bluntly, "Have you ever taken payola?" His question was not coming out of left field. Five days before, the Special Subcommittee on Legislative Oversight of the Committee on Interstate and Foreign Commerce had begun to delve into the issue of payola in the music industry. I told Goldenson the truth, that I had never accepted payola. He asked me about my other music business interests, and I explained that I was a part-owner of two record labels and had started music publishing companies. Although these activities weren't illegal, Goldenson gave me twenty-four hours to decide if I wanted to stay with the network or keep my other businesses. Since I was a kid, I always thought my future would be in broadcasting. I know now that if I had chosen to stay in the music field, my workaholic nature would probably have made me a very successful music publisher, record distributor, and multiple label owner, which ultimately could have been more profitable than remaining in television. But that wasn't where my heart was. I was ready to give up everything else to stay with ABC and *American Bandstand*.

Making that decision didn't guarantee that everything I had worked so hard for was secure. I was still being investigated by Congress. I may have made mistakes and not been a perfect businessman, but as I prepared to testify before the Subcommittee, I knew that I had my honesty and my integrity. But would that be enough? In 1960, we didn't question the government. This was long before Watergate, the Iran Contra scandal, and *The X-Files*. The very fact that I was being questioned by a Congressional subcommittee was enough to darken my image in the eyes of some people. It didn't matter that I had not committed any crime, I was just twenty-nine years old, and the idea that this witch hunt could end my career was very frightening.

The Congressional hearings were covered in the press, so it was easy for me to follow them closely. Months went by before I was actually called. But my name was mentioned frequently in testimony. I was a ripe target for this committee of eight congressmen, headed by Representative Oren Harris of Arkansas. The phenomenon and success of rock 'n' roll had happened because of the efforts of a lot of radio stations, independent record producers, and talent that people had never heard of. I got a lot of the reflected fame because I was the most visible person out there. Hosting *American Bandstand* gave me national recognition, so I got the glory, and I got a piece of the blame. I was also a target because I was young and wealthy.

This same Subcommittee had investigated the quiz show scandals, and now they had rock 'n' roll in their sights. I think the religious leaders who spoke out against the "evils" of rock music were sincere about fearing its influence, albeit misguided. I think the major record companies and music publishers who thought this new music was threatening their livelihoods spoke out because of self-preservation. But the politicians didn't really care about payola or saving America from rock music. They were driven by politics and the desire to get re-elected.

This new rock 'n' roll culture was all about being young and rebellious. The fanatics wanted to nip it in the bud, and the politicians wanted to cater to them. They didn't realize it was too late. Too many people had already been inspired by the passion and freedom

inherent in this new music, and too many people had embraced it as their own for rock 'n' roll to be killed off. I was very proud we managed to survive the criticism, and I was very proud that I stood my ground before the Subcommittee and spoke the truth. I was not charged with anything, but the hearings did leave some permanent scars. I did not come out of the experience a better person—it hardened me, although it did make made me more resilient, and I still think the good guys win in the end. I learned that along the way there will always be a lot of people who have their own agendas, who are very happy to take you down. I also learned a lesson I've never forgotten: you've got to watch your back at all times.

Ironically, the only effect the payola hearings had on *Bandstand* was that our ratings improved and I was more popular than ever. The kids who danced on the show and the people who watched at home didn't really care about the Congressional hearings, and that's why the politicians weren't well-served by their efforts to decimate rock 'n' roll.

The sixties may have started on a turbulent note for me, but most other people were having a different experience. Eisenhower was still president, and families like the

four days in november

The assassination of President John F. Kennedy on Friday, November 22, 1963, was especially hard on America's young people, who in 1963 made up one-half of the U.S. population. Kennedy's own youth, energy, and rhetorical eloquence had inspired them to reach beyond themselves by volunteering for community and government service. By the millions, they joined local and national assistance groups, including the Peace Corps and the Alliance for Progress. From the time the president was pronounced dead in Dallas until he was buried three days later at Arlington National Cemetery, Americans watched in shock as the events unfolded before them live on their TV screens. All regular programming was suspended and all commercials dropped for four days.

ones we saw in *Father Knows Best* and *The Donna Reed Show* were the ones to emulate. In many ways, we were still an innocent nation about social issues, and the music reflected the times. The rebelliousness of Elvis Presley had given way to music with smoother edges. Girls sang about "Johnny Angel" and how they wanted to be "Bobby's Girl," and boys sang about sealing letters with a kiss and crying in the rain. In retrospect, it was the calm before the storm.

Having survived the payola hearings, *American Bandstand* in the early part of the decade still faced two major challenges that could have finished off the show. The first came on August 30, 1963, when we had our final daily broadcast. On September 7, *American Bandstand* became a weekly series, appearing on ABC every Saturday. It wasn't because our ratings dropped. I've always thought the scheduling change happened because station managers missed the point of the show's success. The action was too monotonous for them, and they thought they could find another way to fill the slot. I was concerned with what reducing our airtime would mean for the future of the show. One thing changed pretty quickly; because you weren't seeing the kids who danced on the show five days a week, you didn't care about them as much—they weren't such a big part of your life. The regulars went from being major stars to moderate stars, their fan clubs and fan mail diminished, and they didn't get as much press coverage.

The reduced number of hours we were producing every week had some beneficial effects for me. I didn't have to be in the studio five days a week, so I could go out on the road with our touring show, the Caravan of Stars. We'd have as many as seventeen acts on one bill, all backed by the same band, with me as emcee. The acts would travel around the country on a bus, and I don't mean a fancy, million-dollar touring motorhome. I mean a *bus*. I think one of the reasons I've developed intimate relationships with so many artists is that we shared some very cramped quarters together for days at a time. On the bus, people would sleep sitting up (except for Gene Pitney, who was so skinny he'd sleep in the luggage rack) or we wouldn't sleep at all—we'd stay up all night drinking. When *Bandstand* went to the once-a-week routine, I'd zip back to the studio to do some shows. By this time we had videotape and could produce shows ahead of time, which really freed up my schedule. Then I'd rejoin the tour.

Our Caravan of Stars arrived in Dallas on November 22, 1963. I was travelling with Bobby Rydell, Jimmy Clanton, Brian Hyland, the Dovells, and Dale & Grace. That morning, we watched President Kennedy's motorcade drive by and turn onto Elm Street. We applauded JFK and his wife Jackie, and then went back to our hotel. We were going to work late, so I took a nap. That's why I didn't discover until a couple of hours later that the President had been shot.

Like the rest of the nation, everyone travelling with the Caravan was devastated by the shocking event. In the three short years of his administration, President Kennedy had touched the youth of America like no president before him. Not only was he younger than his predecessors Eisenhower, Truman, and Roosevelt, he had openly embraced the arts and welcomed popular entertainers into the White House. It would have been difficult to picture Ike dancing the Stroll, but not so difficult to imagine Jack and Jackie and Robert and Ethel and all the other Kennedys Twisting the night away, when they weren't throwing each other into the swimming pool. By championing the Peace Corps and promising that America would put a man on the moon by the end of the decade, he created an atmosphere of optimism and instilled America's youth with hope.

It wasn't very long after the assassination of President Kennedy that the music industry was turned upside down by a new group. In order to put our national grief behind us and move on, we needed something brand-new to come along and grab our attention. I don't think anyone *consciously* embraced a new rock group because of Kennedy's death, but the country was ready for something as exhilarating and ingenious as the Beatles. I was already familiar with their song "She Loves You," which had been released a few months earlier on Swan Records, one of the labels I had an interest in before Leonard Goldenson

in the line of fire

Paratroopers from the 101st Airborne division hold their wounded buddies as a soldier guides a medical evacuation helicopter (above). Scenes like this were repeated daily for almost ten years as American troops fought to defeat the North Vietnamese. Not since the Civil War had a conflict so divided America. As U.S. involvement escalated and casualties mounted, the divisions deepened. Students rose up in protest to denounce the fighting. Music played its part in the protest. Phil Ochs's "Draft Dodger Rag" (1965) and Country Joe's "Feel-Like-I'm-Fixin'-To-Die-Rag" (1968) were typical of the movement. For the soldiers in Vietnam, hard rock provided diversion. By 1968, many of the protests had turned violent, forcing President Lyndon Johnson to pull out of the presidential race for re-election.

asked me to give up my businesses. Bernie Binnick and Tony Mammarella kept the Swan label going, but bombed with "She Loves You." I tried to help Bernie and Tony by featuring the single on Rate-A-Record in 1963, but the reaction was unenthusiastic. When the score was averaged, it got a 73, and when the kids saw a photo of the four long-haired lads, they just laughed. The irony is that if Swan had sold just 50,000 copies of "She Loves You," they could have kept the Beatles signed to the label. Years later, I asked Bernie, "Why didn't you just buy 50,000 copies yourself?" He said, "You played it and it bombed. Who was to know they were going to be the biggest group of all time?"

Everyone was to know, but not until Capitol Records released its first Beatles single in December 1963. This time, the label that had passed on earlier Beatles songs in America made the right decision by

releasing "I Want to Hold Your Hand." A buzz had been building on the group in the U.S. for several months while the Fab Four conquered their own country. A Washington D.C. disc jockey obtained a British copy of "I Want to Hold Your hand" from a flight attendant and started playing it on the air. The reaction was so positive that other radio stations began playing the song, and Capitol was forced to advance the release date and increase the press run from two hundred thousand copies to one million.

In forty years of observing pop culture, I have never seen such an overnight change in music. The Beatles were an instant phenomenon, and they had an immediate effect on rock 'n' roll. Before the Beatles, groups rarely wrote their own songs. They relied on the pop tunesmiths of the day, songwriting teams like Gerry Goffin and Carole King, Barry Mann and Cynthia Weil, and Jeff Barry and Ellie Greenwich. After the Beatles, groups became self-contained, playing their own instruments and writing their own songs. Week by week in 1964, the pop vocalists who had dominated the charts in 1962 and 1963 disappeared from the scene. Best-selling artists like Connie Francis, Frankie Avalon, Bobby Rydell, Chubby Checker, and Dee Dee Sharp never had another top ten hit after the Beatles became successful. There were some exceptions—Lesley Gore, Bobby Vinton, and the Four Seasons managed to keep selling records, and the up-and-coming Motown artists like the Supremes, the Four Tops, and Mary Wells all had number one singles.

The Beatles were so dominant in 1964 that one week in April, they captured the top five spots on the national pop singles chart. The following week, they had fourteen different titles on the top 100, something that had never been accomplished before and will probably never happen again. The rest of the chart was filled with British groups like the Dave Clark 5, the Searchers, Gerry & the Pacemakers, the Animals, Billy J. Kramer & the Dakotas, the Kinks, and Herman's Hermits. It didn't matter if a band was from Liverpool or London or Manchester, as long as they looked and sounded English, they were adored.

Because *Bandstand* always presented the latest in music trends, we scoured the United Kingdom to find British groups to appear on the show and to join our Caravan of Stars. We played lots of British music. We showed newsreel footage of the Beatles, covered their press events, and even had contests. One of the road managers for the first Beatles tour of America was Ira Sidelle. Ira had worked with me on the Caravan of Stars, so I called him and asked him to collect any left-over stuff that the Beatles had touched or thrown away. He sent me a boxful and we asked people to write in if they wanted to win some item. We got over a million pieces of mail from people who wanted Ringo's pillowcase or George's cigarette butt.

Later in 1964, I even took a 16mm silent camera to England and filmed a concert starring British groups at Wembley Arena so we could show it on *Bandstand*. You couldn't hear the music on the film, so I described the action on stage. That's how starved we were to know what was happening across the pond, and to hear the jangly guitars, sweet harmonies, and innocent pop melodies that were the hallmarks of the British invasion bands.

What amazed me about the success of these U.K. acts was that they were recycling American music that they had heard on radio while they were growing up. They had been influenced by it and had the smarts to wrap it up in new packaging and send it back to America. We didn't appreciate our own R&B music enough, and a lot of American kids didn't even realize the Beatles were recording an old Isley Brothers song like "Twist And Shout" or that in 1964 the Dave Clark 5 was remaking the Contours's 1962 hit "Do You Love Me?"

Aside from moving to a weekly format, the other major change that happened to *Bandstand* in the sixties was the move from Philadelphia to Hollywood. With the new schedule, my voracious appetite for work wasn't being satisfied, and I knew I needed to be in either New York or California. Hollywood was the hottest place in the country back then. The motion picture studios were based in Southern California, attracting talented actors, writers, directors, and

producers from all over the world. More and more, television production was moving from New York to Los Angeles. It was the land of perpetual sunshine, and it seemed like everyone wanted to be a surfer, whether they lived near the water or not. The music scene was also more interesting in California. The Beach Boys personified the West Coast sound, and L.A. was home to the brilliant producer Phil Spector, as well as up-and-coming record labels like A&M, founded by Herb Alpert and Jerry Moss.

I decided not to call attention to relocating *Bandstand* because I didn't want it to seem like we were making such a jarring change. I know the Philly kids were very disappointed, and it was difficult saying goodbye to them. It was also sad to leave because I had so many close friends in Philadelphia. It was probably the last time in my life I had such an intimate circle of friends. In Southern California people live such mobile lives that you don't get to know your neighbors as well. As a result, most of my friends here are people I've met through business.

In many ways, moving to California was like starting over. I had to find office space, a studio where we could tape the show, and a whole new set of kids to dance on the program. Eventually *American Bandstand* settled into a new permanent home in Studio 55 on the ABC lot at Prospect and Talmadge in Los Angeles. To recruit kids, we went around town passing out handbills inviting teenagers to come over to the studio and dance on the show.

We built a new set in California. The traditional look we had in Philly gave way to platforms of different heights, and the *AB* logo was featured prominently. We had a scrim and could change the color of the set with lights—not that it mattered much, because we were still broadcasting in black-and-white. For the first time, there were network technicians to handle audio and lights instead of the local crews we had in Philadelphia. We felt like we had moved uptown.

One important piece of the set did survive the cross-country move—my podium. Ed McAdam, who started working for me as a bouncer at record hops in Philadelphia and became the road manager for the

Caravan of Stars, drove from Philadelphia to Los Angeles pulling a trailer that contained the podium along with my *Life* magazine collection and my record albums.

Our first show from Hollywood was broadcast on February 8, 1964, and although we didn't plan it, our guest stars were all residents of Los Angeles. Jackie DeShannon was born in Kentucky, but had moved to Southern California in 1960. Dick and DeeDee formed a vocal duo while they were high school students in Santa Monica, where they grew up. They helped give that first show a real California feeling. The guests got an extra bonus out of the move—for the first time, we set aside a half hour for the artists to rehearse their performance before we taped. This was a luxury we never enjoyed in Philadelphia, where we'd bring the artist out, put the record on, and have them lip synch without any rehearsal. Ed Yates, who directed the show in Philly and moved to Los Angeles with us, finally had a chance to do some camera blocking before the show went on air. There's always the danger that too much rehearsal will reduce spontaneity, so we kept the rehearsal short. The other show elements were not rehearsed beforehand, and we continued to tape *Bandstand* as if it were a live show—meaning we started tape rolling and didn't stop until the show was completed sixty minutes later. That's why the show had the same level of excitement and energy.

We were settling into our new home, still caught up in the throes of Beatlemania, when another musical phenomenon caught America's attention. In the summer of 1964, the hottest American sounds were coming out of Detroit, thanks to Berry Gordy's record company. Motown could do no wrong, with artists like the Supremes, Mary Wells, the Miracles, the Temptations, Stevie Wonder, Marvin Gaye, the Marvelettes, and Martha & the Vandellas. They made great records the kids loved to dance to, and we had Motown artists on the show as often as possible.

But there was something even more impressive about Motown. In some fashion, music had always been segregated. There were pop radio stations that catered to white audiences and there were R&B radio stations that catered to primarily black audiences. Lots of songs that started on R&B radio would cross over to pop, but the success of Motown changed that process. These two-and-a-half minute symphonies crafted by black songwriters and producers like Holland-Dozier-Holland, Smokey Robinson, and Norman Whitfield were immediately accepted by pop radio. The songs didn't sound black or white—they were just an irresistible melding of funk, jazz, blues, and soul. They helped break down color lines in America because they were accessible to everyone, thanks to their combustive energy, relentless optimism, and communal themes that touched the emotions of everyone regardless of skin color or station in life.

It was during these early months of Motown's breakthrough success that Berry and I developed a personal relationship, and I called him up in the spring of 1964 to book one of his artists, Brenda Holloway, on the Caravan of Stars. He said we could have her if we'd also take one of his lesser-known acts, made up of three girls named Diana Ross, Mary Wilson, and Florence Ballard. The trio hadn't had any real hit records or appeared on *American Bandstand* yet, so I reluctantly said yes in order to book Brenda. While the Supremes were travelling around the country on our bus, they hit number one for the first time with "Where Did Our Love Go." They moved from the bottom of the bill to the very top in short order, and couldn't believe their fairytale-like overnight success, especially after being dubbed the "no-hit Supremes" by their fellow Motown artists. From this point on, their hits kept coming, starting with an unprecedented five number one singles in a row over the next few months.

The Supremes eventually came on *Bandstand* to sing their 1967 hit, "Reflections," but they weren't the first girl group of the sixties to guest star on the show. The Shirelles, the first female trio to hit it big in the decade, made their television debut when they performed "Tonight's The Night" on the October 19, 1960, show. I loved having Shirley, Beverly, Doris and Micki on the show, but I never realized how young they were because they were so professional. They were just junior high school students when they decided to put a group together.

Time and again, performers who would later became world-famous made their debut on *Bandstand*. In the fifties, *Bandstand* had featured many teen idols, and we continued that tradition in the sixties. Way before he became famous for "Tie a Yellow Ribbon 'Round the Ole Oak Tree," a handsome teenager named Tony Orlando came on the show to perform his hit, "Halfway to Paradise." Unfortunately, while he was singing, his fly was open. Tony appeared on the show many times after that, but he'll never forget his television debut.

Another of the most popular teen idols in the early sixties was Bobby Vee. He was what you call a "closer," the act you bring out at the end of the show to get the girls to scream. He was also a real musician and a gentleman. I even forgave him for coming up to me on my thirtieth birthday party during a Caravan of Stars show and telling me, "You look pretty good for a guy your age." Years later, when he turned fifty, we were doing a show together and I finally had the chance to go up to him and say, "You look pretty good for a guy *your* age." Underneath all the joking, we were both aware of how important image is in this industry. If Bobby had not been a babyfaced, good-looking teenager when he recorded "Take Good Care of My Baby," would it have been a number one single? No matter how talented he was, probably not. As a medium, television has amplified the importance of being attractive, even if we know it is what's inside a person that counts.

Like Bobby Vee, Dion DiMucci was a good-looking teenager who was especially popular with high school girls. He was a frequent *Bandstand* guest, although I particularly remember his appearance on

September 26, 1961, because that's the day he sang his number one hit, "Runaround Sue." Back then, I thought Dion was very shy and reticent. It wasn't until many years later that I found out he was having problems even then with drugs. In 1961, it was unheard of for someone so young to be so heavily into drugs. He cleaned up his act when he got older, and as he matured our friendship grew stronger.

One artist who didn't look the part of a rock star was Roy Orbison. The first time he appeared on *Bandstand*, he hadn't started wearing dark glasses yet, and he didn't look very intriguing. Some years later, he accidentally left his prescription glasses at home and in order to see for an appearance in Alabama, he had to wear his sunglasses. From there, he flew to England to appear with the Beatles, and all he had were the dark glasses. He decided to keep the new image, and he was much more mysterious by the time he returned to *Bandstand* in 1964 to sing "Oh, Pretty Woman."

My association with Chubby Checker goes way back before his first visit to *Bandstand*. He was still named Ernest Evans and was working in a poultry market when he was discovered by Bernie Lowe and Kal Mann of Cameo Records. One Christmas, I decided

a time to sing out

Joan Baez and Bob Dylan, posing before a protest sign at Newark Airport in 1962, defined the folk protest movement of the sixties. The two socially conscious singers emerged as the civil rights movement and folk music revival took over the nation's college campuses. In 1959, Baez debuted at the Newport Folk Festival with Bob Dylan. Two years later, Dylan released his first album, Bob Dylan. His second album, Freewheelin' (1963), featured "Blowin' in the Wind," the song that became the credo for the civil rights movement. The following year he scored again with "The Times They Are a-Changin'." Baez's first hit single, "We Shall Overcome," became a song that inspired civil rights demonstrators.

to send out a record instead of a card. Bernie's new artist could imitate everyone from Elvis to Fats Domino to Jerry Lee Lewis, so he recorded the Christmas greetings for me. During that session, my wife Bobbie said that Evans looked like a smaller version of Fats Domino, "like a chubby checker." The name stuck. Two years later, a couple on *Bandstand* was doing a new dance called the Twist. It was way too sexy for *Bandstand*, and I told our director to get the camera off the gyrating hips before we were knocked off the air. But the Twist was too popular to be stopped, and I phoned Bernie to suggest he get somebody to record something like the year-old Hank Ballard song, "The Twist." Instead, Bernie recorded Chubby doing the exact same song. His version was rushed out and went right to number one. Two years later, when the Twist became popular with adults, the single was re-released and went to number one *again*. It's the only time in history that this has happened, and the record is so popular that Chubby performs it to this day.

Way before he became famous as a Las Vegas headliner, Wayne Newton came on *Bandstand* to sing "Danke Schoen." I had Wayne on the show as a favor to one of my closest friends, Bobby Darin. Bobby told me Wayne was a consummate entertainer, and he was right. I think Bobby saw some of himself in Wayne. Both were multi-talented artists with wide-ranging repertoires. They were crooners who could handle the melodies of Cole Porter and Irving Berlin just as well as folk, jazz, blues, and contemporary rock 'n' roll.

Although it was the producer's job to book the talent for *American Bandstand*, I got involved in the process, too. After I moved to Los Angeles, I went to a lot of clubs to check out talent, and someone told me

to go to the Whiskey-A-Go-Go to see a singer who combined his Louisiana roots with other's people's material, like Chuck Berry's "Memphis" and "Maybelline." I was impressed enough to invite the up-and-coming Johnny Rivers to be on the show in June of 1964.

Another male vocalist we had on the show started out as just another singer, but he became one of the biggest attractions in the world, and is still popular thirty years later. Neil Diamond really put himself into his music —you felt like you were getting inside his head when you heard his songs "Solitary Man" and "Girl, You'll Be a Woman Soon."

While Neil was introspective, Paul Revere & the Raiders were the opposite. They were visual and campy and outrageous, and I thought of them as a musical Marx Brothers for television. They would create mad, crazy routines on the spot, and were like the Monkees before that group hit big.

The first hippie band to appear on the show was the Mamas and the Papas. I loved the sound of their intricate harmonies but when they arrived, I was shocked by their eccentric appearance.

bug-in

Every generation needs to define itself—in style or in the actions it takes: being different is important. Often the difference is made obvious in fads. Thirties kids swallowed goldfish—live. In the fifties, there were hula hoops, saddle shoes, and crinolines. In the sixties, a record number of teenagers were using America's fifty-million automobiles for such rites of passage as the first date and the prom. There were movies: Hot Rod Girl (1956) and Dragstrip Girl (1957); songs: "Little Deuce Coupe" (1963); and a new language—"dragging," "dropping the hammer" (releasing the clutch), and "shutting down" (beating an opponent). Teens used the car, especially the popular anti-status Volkswagen "Bug," for something more than transport (cramming as many people as they could into the pint-sized vehicle (above).

I was used to men wearing coordinated suits and women in crinolines, so I wasn't ready for a group that looked like it fell off the back of a Goodwill truck. They all dressed differently. One was tall, one was skinny, one was short, and one was overweight. They were one of the hottest acts of 1967 with "California Dreamin'" and "Monday, Monday." Although they were based in Southern California when they hit it big, their breezy folk-rock sound was really a blend of different geographic influences.

That same year, we had a group on the show that obviously did not want to be on *American Bandstand*. They were young and hip and they must have felt strange appearing on the same teenage dance show that featured poppier acts like Tommy Roe, Lesley Gore, and Lou Christie. I'm sure they only did the show because their manager told them they had to. Looking back at the Doors performing "Light My Fire," and watching that interview with Jim Morrison, I remember how painful it was to try to talk with someone who desperately wanted to be somewhere else.

Although the Doors were from Los Angeles, they epitomized the hippie, psychedelic groups that came out of San Francisco's Haight-Ashbury area. During the summer of 1967, we had the most famous San Francisco group on *Bandstand*. Jefferson Airplane performed "White Rabbit," and years later when I tried to reminisce with Grace Slick about her guest appearance, she looked me in the eye and said, "I don't remember the sixties."

I don't think she's alone. The innocence of the fifties and early sixties had really started to fade by 1967. Drugs had been part of the music industry for a long, long time, but they weren't prevalent in the general population until then, when mind-expanding drugs were suddenly available to teenagers. People really did tune in, turn on, and drop out, and when you look at what was going on in our country, you can understand why, even if you don't approve of drugs. Race relations were strained, and riots broke out in larger cities such as Los Angeles and Detroit. There was a very unpopular war going on in Vietnam, and authority at home was being questioned for the

first time. There were so many incidents in society of old vs. young, liberal vs. conservative, and black vs. white, and all of this showed up in popular music. (No wonder we sometimes had trouble finding records people could dance to during the late sixties!) There were still songs about love and heartache on the charts, but we also had more thoughtful tunes like Buffalo Springfield's "For What It's Worth," Janis Ian's "Society's Child," and the Rascals' "People Got To Be Free" that commented on relevant social issues.

I do know that I never saw any of our dancers using drugs. Maybe they were smoking grass somewhere else, but we didn't even allow tobacco in the studio. If we had smelled anything on one of the dancers, we would have dismissed them. Once they left the ABC lot, they were on their own. We did have a lot of very, very stoned artists performing on the show, however. There was the time I was interviewing the lead singer of a band and, out of the corner of my eye, noticed that the group's drummer had lapsed into unconsciousness.

Recently, someone asked me if, as an authority figure, I was resented by teenagers. I was never the object of their derision, and I think it's because I didn't side against them. But I was part of the establishment, and a lot of so-called hip and groovy people hated my guts because I was perceived as being somewhat square. There were performers like John Kay of Steppenwolf who understood me as an interesting person, when he could have just as easily put me down. But people didn't see me as an authority figure because I remained apolitical, not taking any positions left or right, liberal or conservative, Democratic or Republican.

I didn't like drugs or use them myself—other than cigarettes, which I gave up, and alcohol. By the time drugs became prevalent in the culture, I was in my thirties, a businessman and a family man, so I wasn't in the demographic slice of the population that was into them. I thought drugs did terrible things to your mind and your body. But I found myself in a somewhat tricky position. If I stopped playing music by artists who took drugs, there wouldn't have been much music left to play. If I made a public stance that drugs were

the path to hell and ruin, I would have been seen as a puritanical figure. The kids would have turned me off in droves. The musicians, their managers, and their record companies wouldn't have had anything to do with me. It was a pragmatic decision to remain neutral. Did I make the right decision? To this day I ask myself the same thing, and I'm not sure what the right answer is. I find it fascinating that the music business is still struggling with the issue, and many well-intentioned people are still not certain of the best way to handle the problem.

Another legacy of the hippie era was the new fashions the kids brought to *Bandstand*, and the new problems they caused. We were long past the day when men had to wear jackets and ties, but we did have to ask the women not to wear pants. We weren't being chauvinistic, it was just that with the men growing their hair so long, when the women wore pants, from some angles you couldn't tell who was male and who was female. And visually, that wasn't very interesting. At least our show was in color by 1967. We were the very last ABC show to start to broadcast in color. We had experimented back in the Philadelphia days, but we didn't have the proper technology, and the show didn't look very good. But by 1968, in the middle of the colorful flower power era, we finally caught up with the times.

There were many things about the last half of the sixties that didn't touch the show directly. *American*

feelin' groovy

Hippies grew out of the chaos that was America following the assassination of President John F. Kennedy and the escalation of the war in Vietnam. They wanted love, instead of war, and self-expression instead of mass conformity. Most of them were middle-class kids from the suburbs. In 1965, writer Hunter Thompson called them "white and voluntarily poor." At the first hippie gathering on October 16, 1965, near Fisherman's Wharf in San Francisco, a few hundred long-haired boys wearing headbands and funny hats (opposite) danced with girls draped in colorful dresses, scarves, and strands of love beads. Many wore flowers in their hair. By January, a similar gathering at Golden Gate Park Stadium in San Francisco attracted 20,000 people who danced to the music of The Grateful Dead, The Jefferson Airplane, and Quicksilver Messenger Service.

Bandstand was a place where kids could come and dance and have a great time, and kids watching at home got to see what the latest dances and styles were and what their favorite artists looked like close-up. It wasn't that we were immune to the riots at the Democratic national convention in Chicago, the Vietnam war, or the assassinations of Martin Luther King Jr. and Robert Kennedy, but in many ways they had no place in the context of *Bandstand*. We were the place where for an hour people went to forget about those kind of things.

Not that we shied away from socially conscious music. The Impressions came on *Bandstand* to sing their racially-themed hit "Choice of Colors" ("If you had a choice of colors, which one would you choose, my brothers?"), and both Three Dog Night and Oliver appeared to sing their hits from the hippie musical, *Hair*. We played songs like "Cloud Nine" by the Temptations, "Get Together" by the Youngbloods and "Everyday People" by Sly & the Family Stone.

By the time the sixties ended, I was glad to say so long. It had been a frightening, exhilarating, dangerous, startling decade on personal and professional levels. Conveniently, the music industry provided a curtain call for the decade. In November 1969, the most popular artist of the last two decades had his final number one hit, when Elvis Presley's "Suspicious Minds" topped the chart. The very last week of December, the most popular American group of the decade had its final number one hit. "Someday We'll Be Together" was the swan song for Diana Ross & the Supremes. And heading up the national charts in November and December 1969 was *Abbey Road*, the final album recorded by the decade's biggest group, the Beatles. Something new would be in store for us in the coming decade. We had no idea what it would be, but to paraphrase Bob Dylan, the times were definitely going to be a-changin'.

dick clark

In 1959, Dick Clark put together his first Caravan of Stars, a rock 'n' roll show featuring some of the biggest names in the business, and booked it all over the country. Like Bandstand, Caravan was integrated, a fact that displeased many people, especially when the show went south. The Caravan performers traveled—and practically lived—in a cramped, uncomfortable bus. Though they weren't glamorous accommodations, the bus was cheap. The performers weren't making much money. The top salary of $1,200 went to the headliner. Most others acts earned $500 or $600 a week. Dividing up the fees after expenses left very little. But there were few venues for rock 'n' rollers in the late fifties and early sixties, and the performers and the promoters took what they could get.

▶ Diana Ross (inset, right) and her big hair try to find some comfort on the arm of her seat in the Caravan bus.

production

caravan of stars

Every afternoon millions of teenagers turned on their TVs to watch American Bandstand. Many dreamed of going to Philadelphia and dancing next to the regulars, but with a studio that held only about 150 people, it was an impossible dream for most. So Dick Clark took the Caravan, its stars, and its music to the teens. Wherever the show went, like Florida, (above) thousands waited in lines for hours to dance and to see Clark in person.

BE-IN

In 1963, TV star Annette Funicello and teen singing idol Frankie Avalon were teamed up for an American International film called Beach Party (below). It was a gentle satire on teenage life on Southern California's beaches, peppered with easygoing, breezy songs. Audiences loved it, and American International churned out five more escapist beach movies in which no one worried about jobs, politics, money, crime, or their futures. Innocent and naïve stories, the films set young hearts thumping while showcasing new talent such as Linda Evans and James Darren.

It's what happens when **10,000** kids meet on **5,000** Beach Blankets!

STARRING

BOB **CUMMINGS**

DOROTHY **MALONE**

FRANKIE **AVALON**

ANNETTE **FUNICELLO**

HARVEY **LEMBECK**

JODY **McCREA**

JOHN **ASHLEY**

ALSO STARRING

MOREY **AMSTERDAM** AND EVA **SIX**

And Featuring

DICK DALE AND THE DEL TONES

★ AMERICAN INTERNATIONAL'S

BEACH PARTY

IN PATHÉCOLOR AND PANAVISION

The Caravan drew huge crowds of teens. In many of the towns, there were no theaters or auditoriums to play in, so Clark and his entourage often squeezed into tiny locker rooms to change and crowded onto makeshift stages to perform. One of the first stops was Atlantic City and its famous Steel Pier (above). By show time, thousands of teens stood shoulder to shoulder in the Marine Ballroom to see Clark host an evening of rock 'n' roll.

HOMEWORK

MR.
"HISTO
F
PG's

RATING SCALE

A = Excellent
B = Good
C = Fair
D = Slow progress
E = Unsatisfactory progress

CAMP

Dick Clark left Philadelphia (but not American Bandstand) for Hollywood in 1958 to play a high school teacher in Because They're Young (1960) (left and above). The film's plot was not unlike that of the 1955 hit Blackboard Jungle. A young teacher is put upon by some of the school's tough kids, makes all the right moves, and saves several lives. While not particularly well received, the film brought Clark nice reviews and was a hit with teenagers who knew him from American Bandstand. One of the things the kids did not see were the two telephone books Clark had to stand on to kiss co-star Victoria Shaw. Clark went on to produce several films and to star in two more, The Young Doctors (1961) and Killers Three (1968).

clean teen movies

American Graffiti (1973)
April Love (1957)
Beach Blanket Bingo (1965)
Beach Party (1963)
Bernardine (1957)
Bikini Beach (1964)
The Endless Summer (1966)
Flashdance (1983)
Footloose (1984)
Gidget (1959)
Grease (1978)
How to Stuff a Wild Bikini (1965)
Jamboree (1956)
Muscle Beach Party (1964)
Ride the Wild Surf (1964)
Saturday Night Fever (1977)
Splendor in the Grass (1961)
A Summer Place (1959)
Surf Party (1964)
Tammy and the Bachelor (1957)
When the Boys Meet the Girls (1965)
Where the Boys Are (1960)
Wild on the Beach (1965)

▲ *Even with her Mickey Mouse Club ears, Annette Funicello (above) was every adolescent boy's fantasy. She was pretty, effervescent, talented, and, for a girl her age, curvaceous. The star of TV's Mickey Mouse Club, which followed American Bandstand every afternoon, she had her own mini-series, Annette within the show. Funicello moved easily into more grown-up roles on the big screen, and her fans followed.*

▲ *Paul Peterson (top) and his on-screen sister, Shelley Fabares, were two of television's "typical" teens who became role models for the baby boom generation. As Mary and Jeff Stone on The Donna Reed Show (1958–1966) they were able to parlay their popularity into several hit records. On the show, they rarely reflected how real teens lived; then again, neither did Donna Reed or mild mannered Carl Betz bear any resemblance to real parents. Their family was as wholesome as most of TV's families: Father Knows Best (1954–1962), My Three Sons (1960–1972), The Adventures of Ozzie and Harriet (1952–1966), and later, The Cosby Show (1982–1992).*

JET SET

▼ At the age of seventeen, perky Patty Duke (below) was the youngest person in television to have a prime-time series, The Patty Duke Show (1963–66), named after her. On the show she played identical cousins, Patty and Cathy Lane. Patty was a typical outgoing American teenager, and Cathy, who was a guest living with the family, was a reserved, artistic English lass. But Duke was up to the challenge. Her considerable experience in television and on stage made her a tough professional who could deliver an audience.

▲ Ricky Nelson (above) was rock 'n' roll's first teenage television star. His father, Ozzie Nelson was a bandleader in the thirties, and his mother, Harriet, a bandsinger. Together with their two sons, David and Ricky, their weekly sitcom The Adventures of Ozzie and Harriet followed the life of an all-American, white, suburban, middle-class family. In a 1957 episode of the show, on the eve of his seventeenth birthday, Ricky sang the song "Teenager's Romance." The next day the record company that recorded the song, was inundated with 60,000 requests for the record.

◄ Edd Byrnes (left) cornered the teenage audience with his portrayal of Gerald Lloyd "Kookie" Kookson III, the hip, jive-talking parking lot attendant on TV's 77 Sunset Strip (1958–1964). The role was not supposed to be a regular gig on the show, but teens, especially girls, inundated the studio with fan mail. Brynes was a young TV personality who successfully crossed over into the music world, at least for a short time. In 1959, he and Connie Stevens, another TV personality scored big with "Kookie, Kookie (Lend Me Your Comb)."

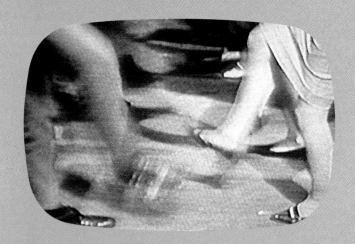

HELLO DOLLY * LOUIS ARMSTRONG

NEEDLES & PINS * SEARCHERS

PLEASE, PLEASE ME * THE BEATLES

THINK * BRENDA LEE

THE WAY YOU DO

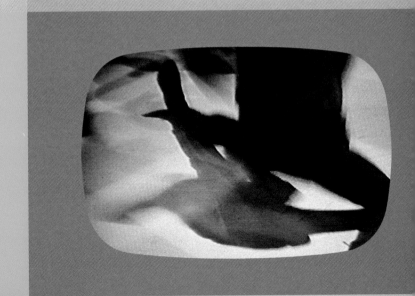

The 1961 Connie Francis song "Where the Boys Are," was about spring break in Ft. Lauderdale, Florida (right). With money in their pockets and car keys in hand, teenagers of the sixties were traveling farther from home for vacations. On West Coast beaches a new phenomena was taking hold—surfing. In 1959, Dick Dale, an avid surfer/musician and Leo Fender of Fender Instruments, created a reverberation unit that came close to duplicating the sound of surfing, giving a distinctive new sound to music. Dale and the Deltones introduced surfing music with "Let's Go Trippin'" in 1961. But it was the Beach Boys who successfully captured the driving, dating, and surfing sixties of teen culture and brought surfing music to America with the hits: "Surfin' Safari" (1962), "Surfin' U.S.A." (1963), "I Get Around" (1964), "Help Me, Rhonda" (1965), and "Good Vibrations" (1966), a single that cost $16,000 and six months to make.

junk foods

Beef Jerky
Bosco
Bugles
Cheeze Doodles
Cheeze-its
Combos
Dairy Queens
Devil-Dogs
Doritos
Dreamsicles
Dunkin' Donuts
Eskimo Pies
Fig Newtons
Fruit Rolls
Gobstoppers
Good Humors
Hostess Twinkies
Hot Tamales
Kool-Aid
Lick-a-stick
Mallomars
Moon Pies
Nestle's Quik
Nutter Butter
Oreos
Peanut Butter Cups
Potato chips
Pretzels
Pringles
Ring Dings
Rocket Push-ups
Slim Jims
S'mores
Snowballs
Yoo Hoo

"Come on baby let's do the Twist!" When Chubby Checker (above) summoned dancers to Twist in 1960, he could never have imagined that the world would actually respond. For the first time since the Charleston, a dance partner wasn't necessary. The Twist began in Philadelphia in 1959 with the release of Hank Ballard's "The Twist." Although the record was only a modest hit, the dance the Philly kids created for it became extremely popular (opposite left). The Twist was banned in many public places because it looked overtly sexual. But teens wouldn't let go. At local dances they Twisted in the center of a circle. By the time the chaperones got through to stop the dance, the dancers were gone, and a new circle had begun somewhere else. When Chubby Checker covered Ballard's record in 1960, the basic movements of the dance, "round and round and up and down," had been set. Chubby did the dance on American Bandstand and it was an instant sensation, putting his version of the song at the top of the charts and making the dance a Bandstand staple.

The most successful girl group of all time, the Supremes, updated the slick, polished sound of the white girl groups of the forties and early fifties by adding glamour and soul. The popularity of black girl groups began with the Bobbettes's "Mr. Lee" (1959) and the Marvelettes's "Please Mr. Postman" (1961). Most of the girls were teenagers and, despite their popularity, had little clout in the music industry. Except for appearances on American Bandstand, few of the groups ever got on national television. Consequently, the girl group craze lasted only four years, from 1964 to 1968. Even Diana Ross and the Supremes, who had twelve number one hits including, "Where Did Our Love Go?" (1964), "Baby Love" (1964), "Come See About Me" (1964), "Stop! In the Name of Love" (1965), and "You Keep Me Hanging On" (1966), went their separate ways in 1970. But no other recording artist or group of the time, except the Beatles and Elvis Presley, had as much success.

Berry Gordy Jr., head of Motown Records, dubbed his headquarters in Detroit Hitsville, U.S.A. (opposite right). By the end of the sixties, a little more than a decade after he started, Gordy had fourteen number one hits and forty-six top fifteen hits. It was the first record company to groom, package, market, and sell the music of black artists to white America. Gordy was a song writer, who after moderate success, started recording and distributing his own songs. The Miracles's "Shop Around" (1960) hit the top of the charts and made Motown a major independent player in the music industry. Gordy's biggest commercial success came during the girl group craze. Among his artists were Martha and the Vandellas, the Marvelettes, and the Supremes.

girl groups

The Angels
The Blossoms
The Bobbettes
The Caravelles
The Chantels
The Chiffons
The Chordettes
The Cookies
The Crystals
The Dixie Cups
Jelly Beans
Martha and the Vandellas
The Marvelettes
The McGuire Sisters
Patti LaBelle and the Blue-Belles
The Ronettes
The Secrets
The Sensations
The Shangri-Las
The Sherrys
The Shirelles
The Supremes
Sweet Inspirations
The Toys

BOUTIQUE

Wherever the Beatles went hordes of screaming girls followed (above). Whether they were in their hotel, at the airport, or in a television studio, it was hard for the boys from Liverpool to escape their fans' frenzy. The Beatles took the U.S. by storm in early 1964, overturning the musical establishment with a sound that was both melodic and hard-edged. But the boys were more than music: they were fashion, art, fad, and put-on. As the sixties rolled on, boys everywhere copied their long hair, their colorful clothes, and their penchant for Eastern meditation. When the Beatles took drugs, the world's young people did too. By 1964, the number of teen and preteen Beatlemaniacs born between 1947 and 1957 numbered forty-three million. The baby boomers, looking for an identity, found it in the Beatles.

Beatlemania was a phenomenon that defined the sixties. As soon as the Beatles's first songs hit the U.S. airwaves, Americans, especially teenage girls, could not get enough of them. Besides their music, the group produced a line of products bearing their name (left). In England in 1963, they sold eighteen million dollars worth of promotional goods. It was these products, plus more personal items, like the towel that Paul McCartney allegedly dried himself with (opposite right), that Clark gave away on a special American Bandstand.

RINGO STARR

GEORGE HARRISON

JOHN LENNON

COACH HOUSE
MOTOR INN

SPEEDWAY INN

PAUL
McCARTNEY'S
TOWEL

THE PILL

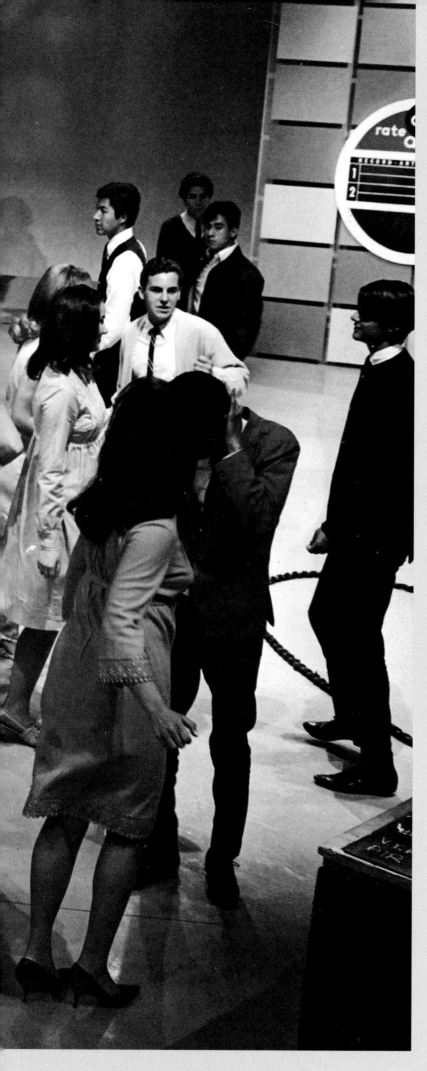

▲ West Side Story was the first Broadway (1956) and movie musical (1961) (above) about postwar teens. It wasn't rock 'n' roll, but Leonard Bernstein's music and Jerome Robbins's choreography captured rock's anxiety and energy. Later, Hair (1968), came as close to rock 'n' roll as Broadway got. With its strong anti-war message and frontal nudity, Hair rocked the Broadway establishment and changed musical theater forever.

◄ When American Bandstand moved to California, a lot more than the location changed. Los Angeles was Surf City, U.S.A., and the show's new set captured the California mood (left). Dancers had more room to move, and guests had more room to perform. Philly regulars were gone, but because the show aired only once a week, this concept had less importance. One carryover from the Philly days was the requirement that the kids be well dressed. Although ties were not the norm in California, Clark insisted that boys wear them. They could leave their sports jackets at home, but if they did, they had to wear a sweater. For the girls, dresses and skirts were still a must.

American Bandstand's first years in California coincided with the British invasion. West Coast kids dressed more casually than their eastern counterparts in the late sixties, but when the hip designers of London's fashion mecca, Carnaby Street, dictated the fashions, even they listened. Stove pipe pants, above-the-knee dresses, and black pointy shoes were the rage. The clothing styles may have changed on the show, but the kids still did line dances based on the old fifties hit the Stroll.

In the early days of American Bandstand, the phone was the principle means of communication between Dick Clark (left), the control room, and his producer. Because the show was always in flux, the order of songs sometimes had to be rearranged, commercials were added or dropped, and facts had to be checked. The phone was the easiest way to get new information. Even when technology made the link to the control room easier with ear pieces and small mikes, Clark still preferred the phone.

Shindig was a big hit for ABC in 1964. With the Shindigger dancers and a roster of top acts, the show, which was performed live, was a solid audience grabber for most of its run (1964–1966). Jimmy O'Neil was the show's regular host, and among his guests who sang live were the Rolling Stones, the Kinks, the Byrds, and the Everly Brothers. The Shindiggers wore fringed dresses and danced in go-go cages (below). NBC tried to counter Shindig's success with a rock 'n' roll show of its own, Hullabaloo (1965–66), but Hullabaloo was a poor copy.

GROK

Born to a famous Detroit preacher, Aretha Franklin (above) grew up surrounded by the best gospel singers in the world. A year after signing with Atlantic Records, Franklin's recording of Otis Redding's "Respect" (1957) hit the airwaves as Detroit erupted into racial violence. From the ashes of the uprising came the expressions "black pride," "black power," and "soul." They stood for black identity, and Franklin's rendition of "Respect," with her "expressive explosiveness," summed up that identity and earned her the title of the Queen of Soul. Franklin is one of the most important voices in the history of popular music. She fused gospel with R & B, threw in some jazz, and added pop. Her unpredictable vocal swoops and leaps defined soul music. Between 1966 and 1969, Franklin had twenty hits, including "Think" (1968), "Chain of Fools" (1968), and "Eleanor Rigby" (1969). She continued to score in the seventies, and in the eighties remained at the top of the charts with "Freeway of Love" (1985).

As late as 1969, kids were still doing the Twist, but throughout the sixties new dances kept surfacing (below and opposite): *the Hitchhike, Swim, Jerk, Funky Chicken, and scores more that remained unnamed. The new dances were like the Twist, in that feet were relatively stationary, and hand and arm movements were emphasized. Dancers mimed movements, like climbing vines (the Monkey), doing the breaststroke (the Swim), thumbing a ride (the Hitchhike) or masking their eyes (the Batman).*

The Beatles's 1967 album, Sgt. Pepper's Lonely Heart's Club Band (right), revolutionized the music business by destroying the single-hit mentality. Before Sgt. Pepper, most record sales were 45 RPMs. Albums, in general, were compilations of unrelated songs. The songs on Sgt. Pepper may not relate in subject matter, but they are linked by feeling and sound. Each song, in which the four singers pretend to be members of the Sgt. Pepper's Lonely Heart's Club Band, leads to the next, and all songs lead to the dramatic final chord. Critics proclaimed it art, record buyers loved its drug-rich imagery and sound, and rock groups began turning out their own concept albums. Except for a few, such as the Kinks's The Village Green Preservation Society (1969) and the Who's Tommy (1969), many of the concepts and the albums were mediocre.

SURFER

When American Bandstand *moved out west it brought with it many of the features that had made it popular in Philadelphia. The Dance Contest was still the most popular feature of the show, and once again viewers wrote in to cast their ballots for their favorite couple.*

DISCO FEVER

We were doing one of our marathon weekend tapings at ABC studios in Hollywood in May of 1974 when I introduced a brand-new release I hadn't heard before. Our producer, Judy Price, thought it was a good record to get the kids moving. I was busy looking at the script to see what was coming up next, but had to stop reading to listen to the music because it was one of the best dance records I had ever heard. "Our love is like a ship on the ocean, we've been sailing with a cargo full of love and devotion." It wasn't Shakespeare, but it had a great beat, and it was easy to dance to. The song was "Rock the Boat" by the Hues Corporation, and it went on to hit number one on the *Billboard* Hot 100, and—along with "Rock Your Baby" by George McCrae and "Get Down Tonight" by KC & the Sunshine Band—it helped usher in the disco era.

In the forty years that I have hosted *American Bandstand* and other musical television shows, I have always declined to answer one particular question—a question I've been asked thousands of times. Everyone wants to know, "What is your favorite kind of music?" It always seemed unfair to reveal my personal preferences as I work with so many different artists and all formats of music. But, I'll break my own rule for the first time ever and reveal that I always secretly liked disco music best. That's not a popular thing to say, because disco is held in such low regard in sophis-

ticated music circles. But I found it appealing; it was happy, frivolous, and lighthearted, and it took you away. Sure, it wasn't music that encouraged thoughtful listening. I played disco music while I worked in my office, because it went in one ear and out the other. The lyrics weren't heavy, and you didn't have to think about them. The music struck me on an emotional level rather than an intellectual one. The secret to disco's success in the last half of the seventies was that people were ready for something light and trifling. In the first half of the decade, we were still burdened with the end of the Vietnam war, the Watergate scandal, and the resignation of President Nixon. It's not a coincidence that a cheerful song like "Rock the Boat" ascended to number one just five weeks before the end of the Nixon presidency.

Music took a ninety-degree turn as the decade began, with many of the artists from the sixties yielding the top portions of the charts to the newcomers of the seventies, like Melanie, Rod Stewart, Don McLean, and Three Dog Night. I began the decade by accepting an invitation from my friend Berry Gordy to attend the final performance of Diana Ross & the Supremes. I flew to Las Vegas on January 14, 1970, and headed directly for the Frontier Hotel. That evening was very emotional for me, watching Diana bow out of the group to begin her solo career. She introduced her replacement, Jean Terrell, and we taped the star-studded evening for *American Bandstand* so the whole country could witness what I could only call, in Supremes's vernacular, a real happening.

As Diana was leaving the Supremes, Gordy was experiencing the first taste of success for his newest group, five young brothers from Gary, Indiana, who

earth first!

The first Earth Day, April 22, 1970, marked the start of widespread awareness of and concern for the condition of the planet. Thousands gathered in New York City (opposite), Washington, D.C., and Los Angeles to speak out for a cleaner environment and stronger governmental programs and regulations to clean up the planet and keep it that way. Many believed Earth Day was instigated by the Nixon White House to undermine Moratorium Day, an annual demonstration in which thousands gathered to call for an end to the war in Vietnam.

called themselves the Jackson 5. The boys made their television debut on *American Bandstand* on February 21, 1970. They performed their first number one hit, "I Want You Back," and for the first time, sang what would be their next single, "ABC," which also went to the top of the chart the week of April 25. What I remember most about their remarkable debut was the stage presence of the eleven-year-old singer, Michael Jackson. Every time I asked him a question, he instinctively took my microphone away from me to answer. Finally I had to say, "Hey Mike, can I have the mike back?" He said "O.K.," and as I asked the very next question, he would seize the microphone again. I broke up laughing and realized this was the way it was going to be. I gave way and the day ended up meaning something much more to both of us; it marked the beginning of a long friendship with the Jackson family.

This youthful quintet may have owned the *Billboard* charts during the early seventies, but another phenomenon was simultaneously taking hold. Thanks to a collection of artists who were tabbed singer/songwriters, music became quiet and more introspective. The trend began with James Taylor and Carole King, who captured the country's attention with hits like "Fire And Rain" and "It's Too Late." The whole music business was especially happy for Carole's success, because she had been writing hit songs since 1960. There were times when it seemed like every song we played on *Bandstand* was written by Carole and her then-husband, Gerry Goffin—hits like "Will You Love Me Tomorrow" by the Shirelles, "The Loco-motion" by Little Eva, and "Chains" by the Cookies. But Carole's *Tapestry* album, released in 1971, brought her to a whole new level of success. The record was number one for fifteen weeks and is still one of the best-selling albums by a female artist. I'm just grateful she included "I Feel The Earth Move" on the album so the kids on *Bandstand* had something to dance to. Have you ever tried shaking your booty to Gordon Lightfoot's "The Wreck Of The Edmund Fitzgerald"? Talented man, great song, but not great for dancing. During those years, we really had to search to find songs suitable to play on the show.

Dancing was extraordinary in the seventies because the kids progressed from making whatever moves they felt spontaneously to choreographing their dances. I recall a lot of dips and twirls, almost like old-fashioned ballroom dancing, very exquisite. Some of the kids even became professional choreographers, like Damita Jo Freeman, who became well-known in the industry when she worked with Diana Ross, the Fifth Dimension, Wilson Pickett, and the Alvin Ailey American Dance Theater. One of the highlights of her career was choreographing the closing ceremonies of the 1984 Summer Olympics in Los Angeles.

Every decade has its own dances. Just like the sixties are remembered for the Twist, the Swim, the Jerk, and the Frug, the most popular dances of the seventies were the Hustle and the Bump. Both inspired popular recordings. Van McCoy's "The Hustle" was a number one smash, and Dooley Silverspoon's "Bump Me Baby" was a dance chart hit that was very popular on *Bandstand*.

The seventies also brought a big change in style for the kids who showed up for our weekend tapings. They knew they were supposed to bring several different outfits, so they could dance on consecutive shows and not look like they wore the same wardrobe from week to week. But the clothes they wore in the seventies were much more outrageous than sixties fashions. I remember one guy who had the strangest platform shoes I'd ever seen. They were transparent and had goldfish swimming around in the heels! When I think about it today, it was inhumane, but back in the seventies it just looked far out. Kids in the seventies were dressed to the nines—they were all peacocks. The kids were older than they were in the fifties and sixties, because we no longer held eighteen as the upper age limit. Some of the dancers were in their early twenties. But age wasn't so important anymore, because the sixteen-year-olds looked mature with make-up and trendy fashions and came off looking twenty years old anyway. This was a reflection of the times—teens looked more adult and more sophisticated; the look of *Bandstand* was bound to change.

The kids who danced on *Bandstand* were still the most important element of the show, and we always made sure they were treated well. Even today, when I see some of the boys and girls who used to be regulars, they remind me how much they enjoyed eating the fried chicken we always supplied for lunch. We also made sure the artists felt well taken care of. A short while back, I ran into someone who now works successfully in the music business. He told me that at one time he had been in a group that didn't amount to much, but it did make an appearance on *Bandstand*. He remembered, "I'll never forget that you came into our dressing room and shook my hand and asked me if there was anything I needed, explaining what we'd probably talk about in the interview. You went on your way, but I felt ten feet tall." He didn't realize it, but that's how I treated everybody. On the shows I produce, the artists come first. I know this is important from years of being a performer myself, with people pulling at me in all directions and demanding things of me when I don't feel up to them. But when you're an artist, you *have* to perform, no matter what. Having been through these pressures, I wanted the artists who appeared on *Bandstand* to have the best experience possible. Even though we didn't have the biggest budget in town, and our dressing rooms weren't the largest, everyone was greeted warmly and we made them as comfortable as possible.

It's also important to take care of your own team. I was the most visible member of the small group of people who were responsible for getting *American Bandstand* on the air each week, but no one produces a television series alone. During the seventies, I put a new team in place that included two people who have been a very important part of my life for the last twenty years. Larry Klein had just moved to Los Angeles in 1974 when he joined our production company as a

give peace a chance

Protests against the war in Vietnam, like this march down New York's Fifth Avenue (above), became commonplace by the 1970s. Dissent reached a fatal peak in May 1970, when National Guardsmen opened fire on a crowd of student protesters, killing four students and wounding eight others at Kent State University in Ohio. Politicians debated how to control civilian unrest, and California Governor Ronald Regan advised, "If it takes a bloodbath then get it over with." Increasingly, Americans of all ages began to question involvement in Vietnam as U.S. atrocities in the Mylai Massacres became public in 1971 and later that year when the Supreme Court ruled that The New York Times *and* The Washington Post *could publish articles based on a secret Pentagon study of the war.*

runner. That's the person who picks up and delivers packages, goes for coffee, or moves desks around if that's what's needed. When Judy Price left her job as *Bandstand* producer to head up children's programming for CBS, Larry became the new producer. He is a truly unique individual whose great asset is his ability to get along with the artists and their managers. Everyone who knows him will tell you they've never met anyone else on the planet like Larry.

hear me roar

As the civil rights movement gained momentum in the early sixties, women were raising their voices, and the world's consciousness, about discrimination against women. In 1963, feminists won a major victory when Congress passed the Equal Pay Act. Then Betty Friedan's book, The Feminine Mystique (1963), let loose with the idea that femininity, and the domestic bliss marriage promised, was a male concept that subjugated women. By the late sixties, activists had organized the National Organization for Women. By the early seventies, feminist demands were amplified by the women's libera- tion movement, which called for sexual revolution. A march down New York's Fifth Avenue in 1971 drew thousands of women (above). Feminists were also heard in music, as exemplified by Helen Reddy's "I Am Woman" (1972).

The other addition to our *Bandstand* staff in the seventies was a young woman who had been working in Washington, D.C., and decided to leave the world of politics for show business. Kari Wigton started work- ing for the head of our business affairs department,

Fran LaMaina. Soon, she was working directly for me, greeting the artists on *Bandstand* and making sure they signed their contracts. If they wanted coffee or something special in their dressing rooms, Kari took care of those requests as well. Sometimes she would give me clues about what to expect from an artist, and how well I might expect the on-air interview to go. But our relationship went beyond working together. I was unhappy in my second marriage, and when it ended, I fell in love with Kari. We moved in together and shared our lives for seven years before we married on July 7, 1977. While our relationship was never a secret, before we were married Kari and I never acted like we were lovers in public. She found it easier to work with the artists as a member of the production staff than as my girlfriend or Mrs. Dick Clark.

Many of the artists we booked in the early seven- ties reflected the swing toward the softer side of music.

The guest roster for 1970 included a brother-and-sister duo from the nearby Southern California city of Downey. Richard and Karen Carpenter performed a lovely song written by Burt Bacharach and Hal David called "Close to You." The Carpenters were as clean-cut as you could get, and their music was intimate, romantic, and understated. Some reviewers made the mistake of dismissing them as being lightweight. The proof that they were wrong has come in recent years, as the artistic depth of their talent has become more critically appreciated. Even in those days you could see that Karen was very, very thin. It concerned me, but we didn't know about her personal problems with anorexia.

A few years later after their first *Bandstand* appearance, the Carpenters were headlining in Las Vegas. I went to see them and their opening act, who was an old friend of mine. Neil Sedaka had a string of hits in the sixties, and made a great comeback in the mid-seventies with "Laughter in the Rain." I had known Neil for a long time, so it was no surprise when he introduced me from the crowd. I was shocked to find out two days later that the Carpenters fired Sedaka for this transgression; they felt it was the headliner's privilege to introduce guests in the audience.

A *Bandstand* tradition of the fifties and sixties continued in the seventies as we presented some of the hottest teen idols on the charts. Bobby Sherman sang "Julie, Do Ya Love Me" on the February 13, 1971, show. He had an ingratiating smile and manner, and girls loved him. He was starring in *Here Come The Brides* on television, so he really had two careers going. Another singer/actor who was very popular with the kids was Rick Springfield, who made his American television debut on September 16, 1972, singing "Speak to the Sky." Rick is a charming, talented Australian, and it was no surprise that he was soon acting in television and films. We had the Osmond brothers on the August 21, 1971, show to sing their number one hit, "One Bad Apple." If there were ever any doubt as to which Osmond was the most popular, you just had to listen to the girls in the audience screaming for Donny. A little over a year

later, the youngest Osmond brother, Jimmy, came on the show to sing his teenybop hit, "Long-Haired Lover From Liverpool." One of the most popular teen idols on the record charts was Shaun Cassidy, the younger half-brother of David. If talent is genetic, Shaun was living proof, as the son of actors Shirley Jones and Jack Cassidy. He sang his number one hit, a remake of the Crystals's "Da Doo Ron Ron," on the April 9, 1977, telecast.

One of the hottest female artists of the early seventies was Helen Reddy, and we had her on the show several times. On May 1, 1971, she made her American television debut when she sang her first hit, "I Don't Know How To Love Him" from *Jesus Christ Superstar*. When she returned on July 29, 1972, I could see some of the teenaged guys in the audience smirk when she sang "I Am Woman." The song may seem dated now, but it was an important statement in 1972 when women were demanding equality in the workplace, in politics, and in relationships. It wasn't the first statement about feminism in pop music— remember Lesley Gore's "You Don't Own Me" from 1964—but it resonated in the seventies. Helen was one of many female artists during this time who stood up for themselves and were known for being independent and strong. Carly Simon, Bette Midler, and Roberta Flack also come to mind.

Al Green touched something primal in audiences, with his gospel-influenced, sensual, falsetto voice. He made his television debut on the October 23, 1971, *Bandstand*, singing his number one hit "Let's Stay Together." Despite his religious background, after seeing women react to him on *Bandstand* and at the concerts we produced with him, I would have never guessed he'd end up being a man of the cloth. He was an electric performer, who was able to transform that power into spirituality when he became a preacher.

If I needed more proof that by the seventies *American Bandstand* had been around a long time, I just had to look at the children of the performers who had appeared on the show in the fifties. They were now old enough to guest star in their own right. Nat King Cole had been a frequent guest during the first decade of *Bandstand*, and at the time, he had me sign pictures to "Cookie" and "Sweetie," his two young daughters. One of them turned out to be Natalie Cole, who made her first *Bandstand* appearance on October 18, 1975, singing "This Will Be." Natalie is a wonderful talent who managed to succeed in spite of having a very famous father. What Natalie did was carve out her own identity first as a credible pop/R&B star. After she was established, she paid tribute to her dad by singing his tunes, "joining him" electronically on duets of "Unforgettable" and "When I Fall in Love."

Another successful offspring of a legend was Debby Boone. It was strange for me to have Debby on *Bandstand* and to ask her about a record that had been number one for ten consecutive weeks, "You Light Up My Life," because I had known her dad, Pat, for so many years, and I had watched her grow up. Even though their biggest hits were separated by two decades, Debby was very much her father's daughter, wholesome and clean-cut.

Barry Manilow was an unknown when he made his debut on the show singing "Mandy," which soon moved to the top of the Billboard pop singles chart. Barry is tall and lanky and may not be the most handsome singer in the world, but he has an enormous appeal to men and women alike, and he quickly became very popular. I know that people have made light of him over the years, but he's a consumate professional, and that alone can make someone an easy target for ridicule. I was especially pleased when Barry wrote the words to our theme song, Les Elgart's "Bandstand Boogie."

One of the most theatrical groups of the decade was introduced to me by Neil and Joyce Bogart. Neil was the P.T. Barnum of the record industry and the founder of one of the biggest labels of the seventies and eighties, Casablanca Records. One of the first bands he signed to his label was Kiss, a hard-rock band that wore white clown make-up and extraordinary costumes, including high heels, and had a singer with an incredibly long tongue who spewed blood. It was great show biz, and kids loved it.

John Travolta was polite the first time he came on *Bandstand*, and he's still polite today. I wasn't a big fan of his Vinnie Barbarino character on *Welcome Back, Kotter*, but I've always liked John as a person. After he sang his hit "Let Her In," I interviewed him and he talked about a TV movie he was filming, "The Boy In The Plastic Bubble." Then, almost as an aside, he mentioned he was doing a disco movie, and that he might turn out to be the "king of disco." He said it so shyly and with so much reserve, I didn't put any stock in his prediction. But, it sure stuck in my mind when I went to see a screening of *Saturday Night Fever*.

If ever a film captured a moment in time, that one did. The first wave of songs like "Rock the Boat" and "Rock Your Baby" gave way to a whole new musical genre, championed by the Bee Gees's "Staying Alive" and "Night Fever." People had always loved to dance, but during the disco era this passion was magnified to the nth degree. And *American Bandstand* was a real beneficiary of this dance craze.

It's hard to step back and assess a moment while you're living it, but looking back on the last half of the seventies now, I realize that *Bandstand* was at its very best. The show looked beautiful from any angle that our director, Barry Glazer, shot it. The lighting was flashier, the dancers were hot, and the music was revved up to 155 beats per minute. It was an incredibly sexy era. Disco was sexy. People were sexy. The sixties may have ushered in liberal sexual mores, but in the seventies everybody was sexually liberated and

the final day

On August 9, 1974, President Richard M. Nixon (opposite) became the first U.S. president to resign from office. His resignation was a dramatic conclusion to the Watergate scandal. After months of investigations and hearings into the break-in at the Democratic party national headquarters in the Watergate apartment complex in Washington, D.C., Nixon admitted that he had obstructed justice by holding back information about the break-in and subsequent cover-up. The Judiciary Committee voted unanimously to impeach him. The scandal—and its revelations about the dishonesty of many politicians and government officials—was a blow to the credibility of the government. The age of cynicism, which had begun with the Kennedy assassination, grew more profound when Nixon was forced to resign.

flaunting it. It was the way we looked, the way we acted, and the way we lived. Having female dancers with slogans plastered across the front of their T-shirts and letting our camera people zoom in on them for close-ups was a long, long way from not being able to say that someone was "going steady" less than twenty years earlier.

The major superstars of the disco era all appeared on *Bandstand*. KC and the Sunshine Band from Florida was a group introduced to me by singer/producer Steve Alaimo, who had been a regular on the TV series I produced in the sixties, *Where The Action Is*. By this time, he was producing hits for Henry Stone, the owner of T. K. Records, home to KC. The horn-driven disco band had five number one singles, and they were always a hit when they appeared on the show.

Six years after Helen Reddy sang "I Am Woman," Gloria Gaynor performed her number one hit, "I Will Survive." It was a feminist anthem wrapped up in disco music, and this time no one snickered. We were making progress on gender issues when a female artist could sing about standing on her own and be taken seriously.

The ultimate disco band had to be the Village People. I loved them because they didn't take themselves seriously. They were campy and crazy, and even though the real Y.M.C.A. threatened to boycott us for having the group on the show, the Village People survived and became American icons because they struck a responsive chord in everybody—black and white, straight and gay, young and old, male and female. I don't know if people realize that *American Bandstand* played an important role in the band's history. It was the kids on our show who first spelled out the letters "Y.M.C.A." with their arms and hands while they watched the band perform. One of our dancers, David Rosney, claims he was the one who started the whole thing, and I have no reason to doubt him. I wish he'd been at the Gloria Estefan concert in 1996, where they played "Y.M.C.A." over the loudspeakers as a warm-up, and 19,000 people spelled out the letters with hands. The Village People still work with us on shows, so I guess I'd better not reveal their deepest secret, that some of the guys in the band are actually heterosexual.

fundamental differences

The Ayatollah Khomeini (opposite) returned from exile to Iran triumphant after forcing the Shah to flee. As leader of the nation's Islamic fundamentalists, Khomeini purged his country of Western influence. On November 9, 1979, Iranian "students" stormed the U.S. embassy in Teheran, captured ninety people, and demanded that the Shah stand trial. Khomeini threatened to try the hostages as spies. In retaliation, President Jimmy Carter froze all Iranian assets in the U.S. and cut off Iranian oil imports. He then ordered a rescue mission that ended in disaster when one helicopter crashed and others missed their mark. It was not until January 19, 1981, when the U.S. agreed to selected Iranian demands, that fifty-two American hostages were released, ending 444 days of captivity.

One disco star was so hot, we asked her to be the first substitute host on *Bandstand*. Truth be told, she wasn't the first, and I was also on the show, so I don't know why we called her the "substitute" host. Disclaimers aside, the honor fell to Donna Summer, one of the biggest-selling artists of the seventies. The man responsible for bringing her back to America after she had gone to Germany to find success was Neil Bogart. He heard her erotic recording of "Love To Love You Baby" and released a sixteen-minute extended version of the orgasmic song. It made Donna a star, and she just got bigger and bigger, closing out the seventies with back-to-back number one hits, "Hot Stuff" and "Bad Girls."

It's no mystery to me why I loved the seventies so much. I was totally reinvigorated during those years. I fell in love and for the first time in my life I was personally happy. I loved the music of the era and was delighted that my good friend Neil Bogart was at the forefront of what was happening. It was one of the best times of my life. But, as great as I felt when the decade ended, I wasn't sad to leave the seventies behind. I was definitely ready for whatever adventures and surprises the eighties held in store.

In Philadelphia, the job of Bandstand's lighting designer was to make sure everyone could be seen. In California, the designer's challenge was to create an environment that matched the feel of the music. With the hippie revolution of the late 1960s had come a new kind of music and a new way to use lights to experience it. Acid rock reflected the mind-expanding drugs popular at the time, and many musicians simulated drug-induced experience with colorful light shows. In Bill Graham's theaters, Filmore East and Filmore West, bands like the Grateful Dead and Jefferson Airplane played center stage while abstract patterns made from colored gels in water were projected on huge screens behind them. As lighting advanced so, too, did the light shows, reaching their apex in the discos of the seventies.

131

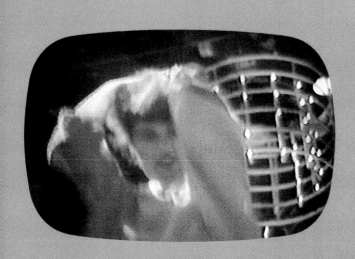

▲ In the frenzied disco scene of the seventies, it was Donna Summer's voice that rose above all others (above). Born in Boston as Donna Gaines, she made her professional debut at the dance club Psychedelic Supermarket in the late 1960s. After a stint in the Munich production of Hair, she released an unprecedented seventeen-minute song about lust and desire, "Love to Love You Baby" (1975). It hit nerves. One of the first female singers to do a synthesizer-pop record, "I Feel Love" (1977), she followed it up with the concept album, Once Upon a Time (1977), and a hit reworking of Richard Harris's megahit song "MacArthur Park" (1978). The song "Last Dance" (1978) was a disco anthem and earned her two Grammys.

◄ Throughout the decades, Dick Clark picked up on new trends and incorporated them into the show. The show's sets were a sure sign of these changes. They reflected the advances in technology, as well as the shift in dance venues, from gyms to discos. By the early seventies, the set (left) reflected life in airy, spacious California. Clark's podium, long a symbol of his place in the show's festivities, was Lucite and small, and no longer separated him so dramatically from the rest of the set. Dancers had more room and more levels on which to do their thing.

environment!

HYPE

▲ Decked out in their Elvis-like jumpsuits, the Osmonds (above, left to right Merrill, Donny, Jay, Wayne, and Alan) won the hearts of teenage girls and middle America. In 1957, they began singing in their hometown of Ogden, Utah, and when they appeared on Andy Williams's weekly TV show in 1962, thousands of fan letters poured in. Their first million selling song, sung in Japanese for that market, made them international stars. Their first U.S. hit was "One Bad Apple" (1971), which was number one on the pop charts and climbed to eight on the R & B charts. Their sister Marie joined the brothers in 1972, and Donny and Marie began their own television series in 1976. In the eighties, Marie went country and Donny went rock 'n' roll, but the Osmonds are remembered as the quintessential all-American, squeaky clean group.

▶ Tony Orlando was working as a music publisher when a friend asked him to sing lead on a new song he wanted to track. Orlando agreed and fronted a group of studio musicians called Dawn. The song was named "Candida," but by the time the record was released in 1970 Orlando had forgotten about it. But then the record climbed the charts to number three. Along with the group, he returned to the studio to record "Knock Three Times" (1971), which went to number one. But because Dawn was still a studio group, there was no one to tour with to promote the song. In 1973, Orlando met Telma Hopkins and her cousin Joyce Vincent (opposite). They agreed to be Dawn, and just before they went on the road, the new group recorded a song Bobby Vinton had turned down, "Tie a Yellow Ribbon 'Round the Ole Oak Tree" (1973). Soon, it became an international hit.

The Brady Bunch (1969–1972) was TV's
first sitcom about a blended family. The
mother, Carol (Florence Henderson), had
three very lovely girls (Marcia, Jan, and
Cindy). The father, Mike (Robert Reed),
had three boys of his own (Greg, Peter,
and Bobby) plus a housekeeper, Alice
(Ann B. Davis). The kids were popular
overachievers, the parents easy-going
hipsters, and the family's problems
solved with reasoning and a good word.
The Brady kids were not known as a
musical bunch, but they did sing on their
show. As a group they appeared on
American Bandstand to promote their
single "It's a Sunshine Day" in 1972.
Their other singles include "Time to
Change" (1971) and "We Can Make
the World a Whole Lot Brighter" (1972).
The Brady Bunch also recorded several
albums, Meet The Brady Bunch (1972)
and The Brady Bunch Photographic
Album (1973).

HATCHBACK

▲ The Village People (above), who appeared on Bandstand in 1977, scored big with the party-going, late-night disco dancers of the late seventies. The original six guys in the group were campy and proud of it. The idea for the group came about because of French record producer, Jacques Morali, who was fascinated by the role-playing costumes worn in some New York gay bars. He hired six singer-actors and put the act together in 1978. That same year they made a splash with "Macho Man," followed by their super hit, "Y.M.C.A." "In the Navy" (1979), was so popular and catchy it almost became a recruitment song until its gay message was explained to Navy officials.

◀ Shoes can be bizarre, practical, elegant, or sporty, but as a fashion statement they always say something about the person wearing them. This pair (left) is a take-off on a 1940s winged-tip spectator shoe. American Bandstand was a showcase for fashion trends from its start in 1957. By the seventies, fashion became costume—outlandish and different. Men's shirts sported long, pointy collars. Pants were flared and often patterned. Pastel-colored polyester suits with built-in belts were the rage in discos.

▼ Heavy metal began when the English group Led Zeppelin (below) turned up the volume on their electric blues and added a macho stage show. Jimmy Page, Robert Plant, John Paul Jones, and John Bonham's first album Led Zeppelin (1969) included old blues songs like "You Shook Me" and "I Can't Quit You Baby," and hit the top ten first in England, then in America. A critic recognizing their unique metallic guitar sound characterized their music as "heavy metal." Black Sabbath followed, and in 1971 Deep Purple went off in a new direction turning out the classic Fireball. The next year, their album Machine Head made the U.S. charts. In the early 1980s, heavy metal mutated into thrash with bands such as Metallica and Megadeath. Van Halen followed with a smoother sound. In the 1980s, Def Leppard and Guns 'n' Roses took the Van Halen sound and made it phenomenally successful.

▲ Dick Clark liked sitting in the Bandstand bleachers. They got him out from behind his podium and put him face to face and shoulder to shoulder with the kids who danced on the show. In contrast to the dancers, who had begun to look older, Clark seemed youthful. In Philadelphia, kids had to be between fourteen and eighteen. When the show moved to California, those rules were dropped, Clark says, because it became increasingly difficult to judge how old a dancer was. In the late seventies, Clark's hair reflected the styles around him (above). He'd also let his sideburns grow or disappear according to the current fashion.

▶ One of the ways teenagers watching Bandstand got to know their favorite dancers was the Spotlight Dance (opposite). Three couples, illuminated by spotlights, had the floor to themselves. It was their chance to shine, to let viewers see just how well they could dance. Unlike the Philadelphia studio, the California studio was large and resembled a high-tech disco.

LIFESTYLE

▲ John Travolta, who first appeared on American Bandstand in 1976 (above), began his career singing and dancing on Broadway in Grease (1973). But in the stage version of Grease he was a chorus boy and few noticed him. In 1975, everybody knew him as the amiably dense Vinnie Barbarino on the TV sitcom Welcome Back, Kotter (1975–1979). Like other young television stars, he was able to parlay his TV popularity into a successful recording career. In 1976, he entered the top ten with the number ten hit "Let Her In." Later he reached the number one spot with "You're the One I Want" (1978). Despite his popularity on television and in music, no one could have foreseen the impact of his performance in Saturday Night Fever. The movie catapulted him into an Oscar nomination and superstardom, and made him an icon of the disco era.

▶ Before Michael Jackson appeared on MTV, the station featured few black artists. But in 1983, Jackson shattered that barrier with the release of three videos, Billie Jean, Beat It, and Thriller. In 1964 at the age of six, Michael and his brother, Marlon, joined their other brothers, Tito, Jermaine, and Jackie to form the Jackson 5, the last major act to benefit from the Motown system. In 1969, the group released "I Want You Back." By January 1970, it was number one on the charts. The song was the first of thirteen top twenty hits between 1970 and 1975. Not since Shirley Temple had Americans been so fascinated by a young performer as they were with Michael Jackson. Jackson, shown in a 1975 Bandstand appearance (right), also had a string of solo hits in the early seventies: "Got to Be There" (1971), "Rockin' Robin" (1972), and "Ben" (1973). His 1979 album, Off the Wall, made him the first solo artist to have four top ten hits from one album. By the mid-eighties Jackson was the most talked about artist in pop music.

Although dancers separated in 1959 to do the Twist, many dances in the early seventies still required some touching, like the Bump. But most dancers were free to interpret the music on their own. In some ways, freestyle was more demanding, in some ways less. People who couldn't dance, or who had no rhythm, finally had a way to express themselves without worrying about specific steps—they were no longer forced to stay off the dance floor. New York's Hip-hop dancers influenced dancing in the early seventies by isolating different parts of their bodies. Other dancers picked up the movements (opposite and above) sending their hips, arms, and feet in different directions.

STREAKING

▶ When the sounds of ABBA or Gloria Gaynor filled the discos of the seventies, dancers lost themselves in the hypnotic beat of the music and the drone of lyrics. What disco lyrics said were of little or no importance. It was the lighthearted, upbeat, rhythmic music that mattered. With high production values—synthesizers, echo chambers, and other electronic studio effects—it was easy, even desirable, for dancers to get lost in the music. While American Bandstand was not pure disco, the show's set, lights, and the disco hits Clark played were enough atmosphere to carry dancers away (right).

◀ Few films had as much influence on a generation as John Badham's 1977 Saturday Night Fever (left). The film follows Brooklyn paint salesman, Tony Manero (John Travolta), as he moves from his dreary day job to competing at the local disco. The soundtrack album, featuring five songs by the Bee Gees, sold more than thirty million copies worldwide. And the film's dances, choreographed by Broadway's Lester Wilson, were soon learned and copied by every disco dancer. Travolta, in his wide-lapeled suit and open shirt, established the prototypical look for disco dancers around the world.

▶ The discotheque began in Paris, but it wasn't until New York's gay clubs started playing non-stop dance music that the idea caught on. Arthur's (right), was one of the first mainstream discos to draw large crowds. But in disco clubs, music was not the centerpiece, dancers were. Spotlights bathed them in color, falling confetti stuck to their sweaty bodies, and, in many places, drugs heightened, or dulled, their senses. Manhattan's Studio 54, the preeminent dance palace of the seventies, had the most advanced light and sound system and more than 450 special effects, from plastic snow to perfumed mist. Stars and celebrities glided through the doors to crowd onto the surprisingly small dance floor. The music was loud, heavy, constant, and the heat was intense. Co-owner Steve Rubell described his club as an "adult Disney World." By the end of the decade there were approximately 20,000 discos in the U.S.

By the late seventies, TV technology had taken a tremendous leap forward. Although cameras were still large and somewhat bulky, they were no longer hard to push around. Cameramen (below) easily roamed the studio following dancers wherever they went.

WE GOT THE BEAT

John Mellencamp was the first *American Bandstand* guest of the new decade. He was on the charts with his initial hit, "I Need a Lover," which he performed on the show January 5, 1980. As I looked out at the youthful faces of the kids that day who were dancing to Michael Jackson's "Rock With You," I had this sudden, sobering thought. When I hosted *American Bandstand* for the very first time, none of these kids was even born yet! The thought gave me pause. I may have made the transition from older brother to father figure rather gracefully, but in that instant, for the first time, I felt *grandfatherly*. Later in the decade, I would have to think about my age and even consider stepping down as host of the show.

When *American Bandstand* was live everyday for two and a half hours in the fifties, you never knew what was going to happen next. Such spontaneity could have been easily lost when we switched to videotape, but we made a point of shooting *Bandstand* as if it were a live show, taking exactly two minutes for commercial breaks, and never stopping tape for anything, short of a life-and-death emergency.

We had an emergency of sorts in the spring of 1982 when the husband-and-wife duo Nick Ashford

via satellite

By the 1980s, the music industry was truly global. Not only were tapes and cassettes marketed worldwide, radio signals and music videos were bounced by satellite from city to city, country to country, and continent to continent. United States space shuttles, like the successful Challenger (opposite), routinely carried advanced satellites into space. The Challenger's explosion in January 1986, however, watched by millions of television viewers, was a shocking reminder of the limits of science and of our frailty. The explosion devastated young people who believed that America's scientific know-how was invincible. For the first time, many had to face the fact that human error was possible even in the most controlled situations.

and Valerie Simpson arrived at ABC to sing their latest hit. Nick and Valerie are a strikingly beautiful couple who have written some of the biggest hits of the last twenty-five years, like "Ain't No Mountain High Enough," "You're All I Need to Get By," and "I'm Every Woman." They were frequent visitors to *Bandstand*, but when it came time for them to perform their song on this particular day, we couldn't find Valerie, so we had to stop tape. Our producer, Larry Klein, rushed from backstage to tell me Valerie was locked in the bathroom of her dressing room—the door was jammed. Larry called the fire department, and someone showed up with an ax to free her. To Valerie's credit, she was only hysterical for a few moments before she quickly regained her composure. I bet people watching at home wondered why the kids on the show gave her such a huge round of applause when she came out on to the set that day.

The eighties were full of surprises. Some were wonderful and some less so. The sudden demise of disco music was one that caught us all off guard. One moment disco was the hottest thing going, and then, just as the new decade began, it was over. People have offered all kinds of theories as to why disco died. Some think it was a homosexual backlash, because the music was so closely identified with the gay community. Others think people were burned out on artists like the Bee Gees, who dominated the charts in the late seventies, and still others think people were unhappy because rock 'n' roll wasn't getting enough airplay on radio. Disco may have been dead and buried, but I knew that people were dancing long before disco— even long before *American Bandstand*. Sure enough, after a brief respite, the music filled the disco void, only we called it "dance music."

While the days of the Stroll and the Swim were long gone, kids in the eighties found new dances to try on *Bandstand*. In 1984, a fad called Breakdancing caught on. This centrifugal force-based form of dancing, which requires a great deal of strength and athletic prowess, started in the South Bronx and became popular after it was shown in the film *Flashdance*. Two years later, a more sensual form of dancing—dirty dancing—became popular. It was inspired by the movie of the same name, starring Patrick Swayze. This so-called "dirty dancing" wasn't really dirty; even the movie was rated PG. But I thought our broadcast standards editor from ABC was going to have a fit when he heard we'd be "dirty dancing" on the show. Still, if the teenagers of the sixties could have seen the suggestive bumps and grinds of dirty dancing, they'd wonder why I had been reluctant to show the Twist on camera, a dance that by comparison has all the innocence of children scampering on the playground.

One of the saddest moments of the decade took place in December 1980. Kari and I had just attended an Emmy dinner in New York where the the Academy of Television Arts and Sciences had presented an award to *American Bandstand*. As we moved outside into a crowd of people, someone walking down the street noticed me and said, "It's a shame about John Lennon, isn't it?" I answered, "What are you talking about?" and that's when he told me the shocking news of the ex-Beatle's murder. I felt a rush of emotions and Kari and I hurried back to our apartment to watch the news, and to think about the kind of world we were living in. I know John's death had an impact on millions of people all over the world, but it especially impacted other artists; they not only grieved for a fellow musician, they also became security conscious. In the years since Lennon's death, I've noticed that artists have more body guards around them, and that they take even more precautions when travelling than they once did.

The nation turned more conservative in the new decade—witness the election of Ronald Reagan as president. But I don't think this rightward turn showed up on *Bandstand*. The fashions were still outrageous, even if the bell-bottoms, wide lapels, white disco suits, and Afros of the seventies were passe. Along with influencing dance in the 1980s, the movie *Flashdance* also started a fashion trend—the torn t-shirt. It seemed that every girl who saw Jennifer Beals in the movie went right home and ripped up one of her t-shirts. There was also a lot more colorful clothing in the eighties, especially when it came to what men wore. The formal, nondescript look that allowed men to fade into the woodwork was gone, as was the tuxedoed, elegant look of the disco era. It was during the eighties that pants got tighter and men couldn't fit anything in their pockets, so they started carrying purses like women. The biggest problem we had on *Bandstand* with this fad was not having our cameras avoid any obvious bulges, but having to worry about the safety of women's personal belongings. Now we had to be concerned about those of men, too. Thankfully, the trend passed quickly.

Another change that crept up on us was the end of sexual freedom. The inhibitions of the seventies resurfaced as we became aware that sex could kill. It wasn't an immediate awareness, and it took a lot to get our attention. At first the media called the new sexually-transmitted disease Gay Related Immunity Defiency, or GRID. But when they learned more about it, they changed the name to Acquired Immune Deficiency Syndrome, or AIDS.

My experience with this terrible disease is a lot like everyone else's. At first, you think AIDS only happens to people who are far removed from you. Then the disease hits a little closer to home. For those of us who work in the entertainment industry, the death of Rock Hudson was a very loud wake-up call. Over the years, many of the *Bandstand* dancers have been homosexual. And in the eighties a lot of our male dancers were gay, more openly than kids on the show in ealier decades. But it wasn't until someone very close to me died—one of the regulars on the show from the seventies, Johnny Contreras—that I reacted emotionally, and not intellectually, to AIDS.

If you watched *Bandstand* during that time, you saw Johnny dance with his partner, Linda Blythe. They were dance contest winners and often appeared in the Spotlight Dance. They were so professional that Larry Klein asked them to dance in our *Good Ol' Rock & Roll* show, first in Las Vegas, then in other cities. Johnny was someone I knew well and cared about very much, and like everyone else who succumbed to AIDS, his death was a terrible loss to his family and his friends.

The AIDS epidemic increased public awareness of gays in at least two ways. The media paid a lot of attention to the disease, and more gay people, faced with life-and-death issues, came out of the closet and told the truth about their sexuality. That explains why, in this decade, openly gay artists first appeared on the show. Boy George was the flamboyant lead singer of Culture Club, while Neil Tennant and Chris Lowe were two fellow Brits who formed the Pet Shop Boys. Both groups were part of a new wave British invasion that took hold of the American charts in the early eighties. Maybe disco was out, but these groups were making great dance music, much of it synthesizer-based. The sound was a merger of pop and punk that owed much to the British beat groups of the early sixties. The bands that defined this sound included the Human League ("Don't You Want Me"), ABC ("The Look of Love"), and A Flock of Seagulls ("I Ran (So Far Away)"). They pumped new energy into music and made the *Bandstand* producer's job of finding dance records a lot easier.

As in previous decades, some of the most popular artists of the eighties made their television debuts on *American Bandstand*. Three weeks after John

in memorium
When the Names Project first displayed the AIDS quilt (above) in Washington, D.C., in 1987, it was made up of 1,920 panels. In 1992, it contained more than 20,000 panels, and in 1996, close to 40,000 panels, each a memorial to a person who had died of AIDS. By the nineties, AIDS was the leading cause of death in males under the age of twenty-five. AIDS brought out the best and worst in society: people infected with HIV were discriminated against, beaten, and in several cases, killed. But there was also an outpouring of support, especially from the entertainment and music industries.

Mellencamp made his first appearance on our show, a young genius from Minneapolis made his network debut. His name was Prince, and he sang his first hit, "I Wanna Be Your Lover." Over the years, people have commented on the interview I did with Prince after his energetic, erotic performance. When I asked him about the kind of music coming out of his hometown, he seemed to be nervous, fidgety, even sarcastic. When I asked how many years earlier he had made his first demo, he didn't answer; he held up four fingers. The man next to me was such a contrast to the artist who had been grabbing his crotch a few moments earlier that some people took his attitude for rudeness. But I was standing inches from him, and I can tell you he was one of the most incredibly shy, awkward people I have ever met. As someone who is more comfortable in a television studio than in a social setting, I related to this apparent contradiction and understood what he was experiencing. Prince and I have since had conver-

sations and worked together, and I've always been impressed with this very complex man who composes, produces, arranges, plays all of the instruments on his records, and still finds time to work with other artists.

When we taped our first batch of shows for 1984, we featured two up-and-coming female artists who were making their first network TV appearances. It was fascinating to watch them watching each other, each one standing offstage, while the other performed. Madonna hadn't had her first top ten hit yet, but there was a buzz in the studio before she arrived. She walked in without any entourage. When director Barry Glazer was ready to rehearse, she said, "I don't want to do it this way. I want to make an entrance. Would you mind? It would be better for the camera. It would be better for me." We didn't mind at all. All you had to do was watch the audience's excited reaction to Madonna that day, and it was clear this woman—displaying a bare midriff, an armful of bracelets, and crosses dangling from her ears and around her neck—was going to be a superstar.

The other female artist making her television debut that weekend was Cyndi Lauper. The first thing you noticed about Cyndi was the color of her hair, then her bizarre outfit, and finally, her voice. And,

helping hands

With a reawakened sense of 1960s social consciousness, musicians in the 1980s volunteered their talents to raise money for social causes. In 1985, when drought in Ethiopia caused one of the worst famines in history, musician Bob Geldof organized Live Aid, a live concert held simultaneously in London and in Philadelphia (left). Live Aid inspired other charity concerts by the Grateful Dead (save the rain forests); Bruce Springsteen and Peter Gabriel (Amnesty International); Steve Van Zandt (anti-apartheid); John Mellencamp and Willie Nelson (Farm Aid—to benefit U.S. farmers). It also inspired Harry Belafonte to form U.S.A. for Africa which released the star-studded song "We Are the World" (1985).

she had magnificent skin that every woman would die to have—pure, flawless. She was also passionate about women's rights and extremely intelligent. Some people were deceived into thinking she was some street kid from New York who wasn't too bright because of her accent and demeanor, but nothing could be further from the truth. The only thing about Cyndi I never understood was her love of professional wrestling.

Lionel Richie appeared on *Bandstand* as a solo star in the eighties after performing on the show in the seventies as part of the Commodores. When the Commodores were starting out, Lionel wrote and sang their beautiful ballads and was getting all of the attention. It was a thrill to see him grow as an artist and reach the point where he was the star of the 1984 Olympics closing ceremony, singing "All Night Long" to millions of people all over the world. Lionel is very wise, warm, and charming, and we've had a lot of fun times together socially. His only fault is that he's always late. I used to tease him that we'd tell him to be at the studio two hours before we needed him to make certain he'd be there on time.

On January 23, 1982, the Go-Go's made their network television debut on *Bandstand*, performing their first two hits, "Our Lips Are Sealed" and "We Got the Beat." I always loved the Go-Go's because they were so serious about their music. They were not frivolous; being an all-female band was not a gimmick for them.

On March 5, 1983, we had another television first with the American debut of Wham! Looking back at that clip today, it's amazing to see the babyfaced, nineteen-year-old George Michael. What puzzled me while watching them perform "Wham Rap" was why they were a group at all, when obviously George Michael was a solo act. I couldn't figure out what Andrew Ridgeley's role was. George must have asked himself the same question before calling a halt to Wham! in 1986 and going solo.

The April 28, 1984, show marked the television debut of a New Jersey band Bon Jovi. They performed "Runaway" and "She Don't Know Me" from their first album. What has impressed me the most about the group over the years is that no matter how big they've become, they've always been there for me. Whenever I've called Jon and said, "I'm in a bind, I need a group for a show, can you help me?" he always has—all that loyalty just from being booked on a simple little dance show when they were starting out.

In the early eighties, I produced a movie called *Remo Williams: The Adventure Begins*. My son Duane, who writes and produces films, was a production assistant on this project. During production he came home with a friend who had written a rap song for the soundtrack. I have to admit I never saw the rap trend coming. To give you an idea of how much I missed the boat on rap, I told him, "There are two things wrong here: Rap music probably won't be around by the time the picture is released, and I don't know too many white guys who write rap songs." As Duane has reminded me, I was wrong on all counts, and rap is one of the best-selling categories of music today. It's sure done a lot better than the film.

I don't think anyone could have predicted what would happen to the six teenagers who made their first *Bandstand* appearance on September 1, 1984. New Edition was hot. Their song, "Cool It Now," topped the *Billboard* R&B chart. They also had a song called "Boys to Men," and that's exactly how we've seen them grow, from teenagers to adults. They were very excited about singing on *American Bandstand* and returned to the show, as well as other programs we've produced, together and as individuals. It's hard to think of an outfit other than the Beatles where all of the members were successful outside of the main group, but New Edition was. Bobby Brown, Johnny Gill, and Ralph Tresvant have all had big hits as solo acts, and Ricky Bell, Michael Bivins, and Ronnie DeVoe had a number of top ten singles as Bell Biv DeVoe.

Back in the seventies we used to produce concerts with the Jackson 5 and other groups. The Jackson brothers would drag their little sister Janet along, and that's how I met her. The first time I saw Janet perform was on *The American Music Awards* when Michael brought her out to do a Mae West impression. She was only seven years old. She was such a

cute little thing as she strutted down a flight of stairs with a feather boa wrapped around her. As a teenager, she pursued acting, and although she was successful, she decided to go into the "family business." She signed with a major label, A&M, and after a couple of youthful efforts, teamed up with top-notch producers Jimmy Jam and Terry Lewis and produced a mature, dynamic album titled *Control* (1986). Since then she's racked up more than a dozen top ten hits and sells millions of albums.

I felt a special kinship and warmth for John Lennon's son Julian when he came on *Bandstand* to sing his first hit, "Valotte" (1984). Knowing that my kids Rac, Duane, and Cindy have had to deal with the problems of following in the footsteps of a famous father, I was thrilled that Julian was doing so well on his own and that he had established a distinct identity as a songwriter and performer.

The eighties gave us a lot of wild acts, like Devo, but I think the artist who gave us the most memorable performance of the decade was John Lydon, a.k.a. Johnny Rotten of the Sex Pistols. He was in a group called P.I.L., Public Image Ltd., when he appeared on the May 17, 1980, show. Before his group went on stage, he warned me he wasn't going to lip-synch, and that if I didn't let him act as he pleased, he would cause trouble. I told him that as long as he didn't hurt anybody, he could do whatever he wanted. Sure enough, he grabbed kids out of the audience to join the group on stage, put nosedrops up his nostrils— then let the fluid run out, commandeered my podium, and ran all over the studio. It was controlled anarchy. It was also great television. As far as I'm concerned,

the cold war ends

East German border guards look on as a demonstrator hammers away at the Berlin Wall (opposite). On November 9, 1989, tens of thousands of East and West Berliners gathered along and on top of the wall to celebrate the opening of the Berlin border for the first time since 1961. For weeks prior to the collapse of the wall, East Germans marched by the hundreds of thousands demanding freedom and access to the West. They were hungry for consumer goods. They wanted jeans, coffee makers, and other U.S. products. And, they wanted rock 'n' roll. When the gates to the west finally opened, young people streamed to record stores in West Berlin. Within weeks of the border opening, Pink Floyd mounted an all-star concert of its popular The Wall, drawing thousands to the rock 'n' roll extravaganza.

an artist can do practically whatever they want on stage if they drop the act when the camera is off.

We added various elements to the show in the eighties. For a while, we had stand-up comedians do three-minute bits, and we featured music videos on a regular basis. Of course, playing videos took us back to the earliest days of the local *Bandstand* in Philadelphia, when the show was made up of filmed segments of musical artists. In the sixties we showed Beatles videos, and Michael Jackson was one of the first performers to tell me that the Jacksons had made a film of their song "Can You Feel It," a far-out, strange interpretation, that we showed on *Bandstand*.

In 1987, I had to make one of the most difficult decisions of my career. ABC wanted to cut the show down to a half-hour. Rather than give up half of our time, I decided to put *Bandstand* into syndication. We revamped the show, changed the set, the logo, and even the title to *The New American Bandstand*. One problem with syndication is that a show can be on in a different time period in each city. Lots of local stations signed on for *Bandstand*, but many of them didn't run it in its traditional Saturday spot. In some cities, we were on at three in the morning. Because of that, and for a lot of other reasons that had to do with the business of television, *Bandstand* only made it through one year in syndication.

However, I wasn't ready to let go of the show, so we tried another tack. We made a deal to put the show on cable. And, that's when I made the toughest decision of all—to step down as host. The truth is, that in all of the years I hosted *American Bandstand*, I could never visualize anyone else doing my job. The move to cable happened around the time I turned sixty, and I never wanted to hear anyone say, "You're too old for this." I know that I've been dubbed "America's oldest living teenager," and that's a difficult title to maintain. I look in the mirror or see photographs of myself, and I know I'm getting older. However, people who grew up with me don't want to think of me aging, because it reminds them that it's happening to them. I'm trying to age gracefully, but doing so in the public eye is difficult. So, in my heart, I knew that if the show was going to continue, it was time to find a new host.

A talent search led to our own office in Burbank, where David Hirsch, a production assistant on another cable show we were producing, *Camp Midnight*, won the job. To begin, the two of us sat down, and I told David everything I could think of about being the host. Then we did some dry runs and critiqued his work together. It was a difficult process for both of us. At first, I visited the set and stayed in the background, consciously never standing in his line of sight. While it was incredibly hard to watch David take over and do things his way, it was the only way the two of us could continue. Finally I told him, "I've got to back away, because you shouldn't be the puppet, and I shouldn't be the puppeteer." I stopped going to the set after a while so he could chart his own course.

Unfortunately for David and our staff, the show was produced under very difficult conditions. Our "set" was an outdoor area at Universal Studios in Hollywood, and it was either ususally rainy or hot and smoggy when we went to tape. The situation was a real nightmare for Barry Glazer, the director. If you view the shows we produced in the studio just before moving to cable, they had a full, rich, colorful look. We used interesting camera angles, dramatic lighting, as well as different tiers on the set—in short, lots of pizazz—that was all lost when we shot the show in broad daylight. The finished product didn't look very good, and it certainly didn't meet the standards of *American Bandstand*. We weren't very far into our year on cable when we realized doing the show this way was a mistake, and that the time had come to say goodbye to *American Bandstand*, the longest-running variety series in the history of television.

But, I don't think we've seen the last of *Bandstand* as a piece of American culture. People approach me all the time about bringing the show back, and I wouldn't be surprised to see it on television again someday. We're already gearing up for a feature about *American Bandstand*. The show lives on in reruns, and the name also lives on in restaurants. The American

money! money! money!

Between 1984 and 1987, the Dow Jones Industrial Average rose 150.6%, making it the second biggest bull market of the twentieth century. It was the roaring eighties, and Americans were spending money and using their credit cards in record numbers. The Chicago Mercantile exchange traders (opposite) were making money, too. People prospered on junk bonds and leveraged buyouts. But in 1987, the financial markets came crashing down when the Dow dropped 508 points in one day. Traders sold in a frenzied panic. Not all Americans lived the high life in the eighties, however; during this time, the chasm between rich and poor grew. America's conspicuous consumption also led to the highest budget deficits in the history of the nation.

Bandstand Grills are filled with memorabilia from years of rock 'n' roll and *Bandstand*.

Whatever *Bandstand*'s fate, I'm grateful for my health, happiness, and good fortune, and I know that the show has affected every moment of my life. I've treated *Bandstand* like one of my own children. I've nurtured it, watched it grow from infancy to childhood to adulthood. It's given me a connection to the millions of people who watched and enjoyed it through the birth of rock 'n' roll, the arrival of Elvis Presley, the success of the Beatles, the excesses of the disco years, and the rise of today's stars like Madonna, Prince, and Michael Jackson.

American Bandstand. It's got a great beat, and it's easy to dance to. Thanks for watching. For now, this is Dick Clark . . . so long.

If clothes were costumes in the seventies, dance was performance in the eighties. Disco brought back touch dancing with a
vengeance, but it was different; it was athletic (above). At
parties or at local dances, couples in the eighties did variations
of the Salsa and Hustle, like the Latin or the New York Hustle.
The variations were as intricate and rhythmic as the dances of
the forties and fifties (the Jitterbug and the Mambo), and
because of the newly added athleticism, they were often choreographed and rehearsed. The dancers and the dances on American
Bandstand in the eighties took on a professional look, no longer
reflecting kids off the streets but young people who were savvy
about television and the visual arts.

top hops

Alligator	Jerk
Barefoot	Jitterbug
Bird	Kangaroo
Boogaloo	Latin Hustle
Bop	Limbo
Boston Monkey	Lindy Hop
Breakdance	Loco-Motion
Bristol Stomp	Madison
Bump	Mashed Potato
Bunny Hop	Monkey
Calypso	Mouse
Cha-lypso	New York Hustle
Chicken	Peppermint Twist
Circle	Philly Dog
Continental Walk	Pogo
Crawl	Pony
Duck	Popeye
Electric Boogie	Shag
Fish	Shake
Fly	Shimmy
Freddie	Skate
Frug	Slop
Funky Broadway	Strand
Funky Chicken	Stroll
Grind	Swim
Hand Jive	Twine
Harlem Shuffle	Twist
Hitchhike	Waddle
Horse	Walk
Hully Gully	Watusi

During Bandstand's Philadelphia days, a Spotlight Dance on the show's small studio floor could feature three couples at a time dancing side-by-side. On the larger multi-level California set of the 1980s, spotlight couples were featured on platforms and towers. The vertical set allowed kids to dance on several levels (above). When couples danced on the platforms, they looked like dancers in go-go cages which were then popular in clubs around the country.

SUPERSTARS

163

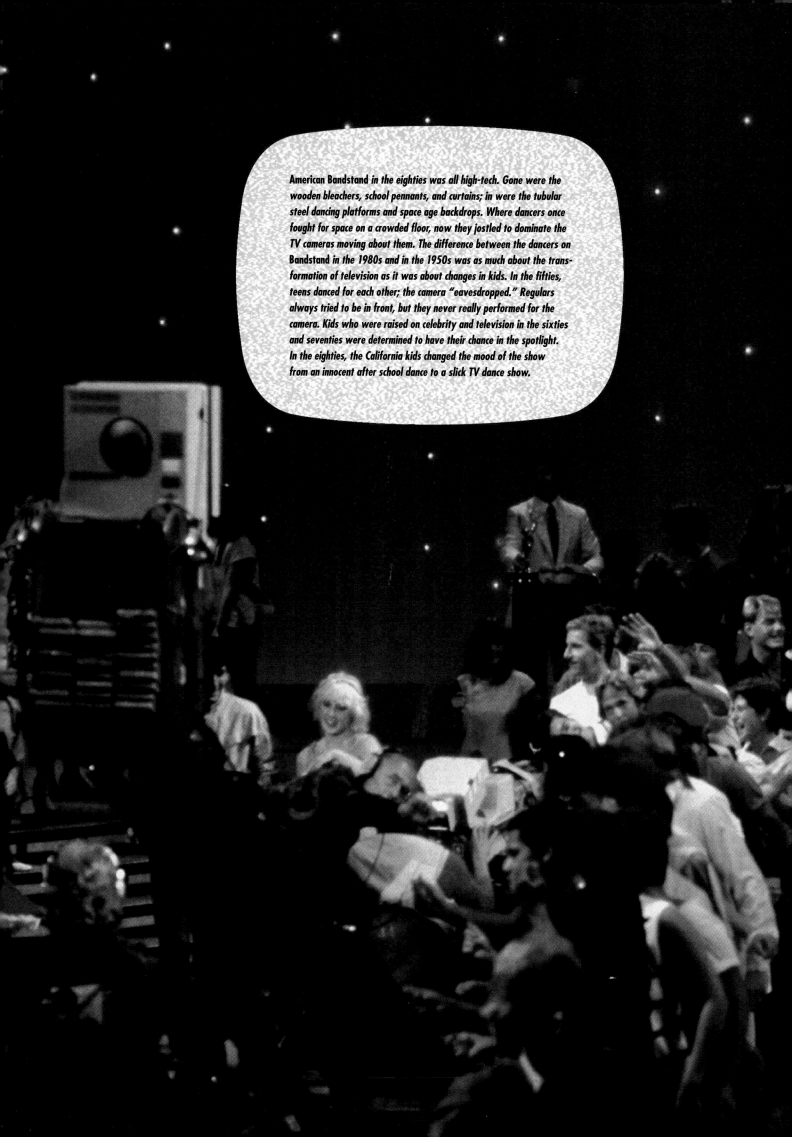

American Bandstand *in the eighties was all high-tech. Gone were the wooden bleachers, school pennants, and curtains; in were the tubular steel dancing platforms and space age backdrops. Where dancers once fought for space on a crowded floor, now they jostled to dominate the TV cameras moving about them. The difference between the dancers on* Bandstand *in the 1980s and in the 1950s was as much about the transformation of television as it was about changes in kids. In the fifties, teens danced for each other; the camera "eavesdropped." Regulars always tried to be in front, but they never really performed for the camera. Kids who were raised on celebrity and television in the sixties and seventies were determined to have their chance in the spotlight. In the eighties, the California kids changed the mood of the show from an innocent after school dance to a slick TV dance show.*

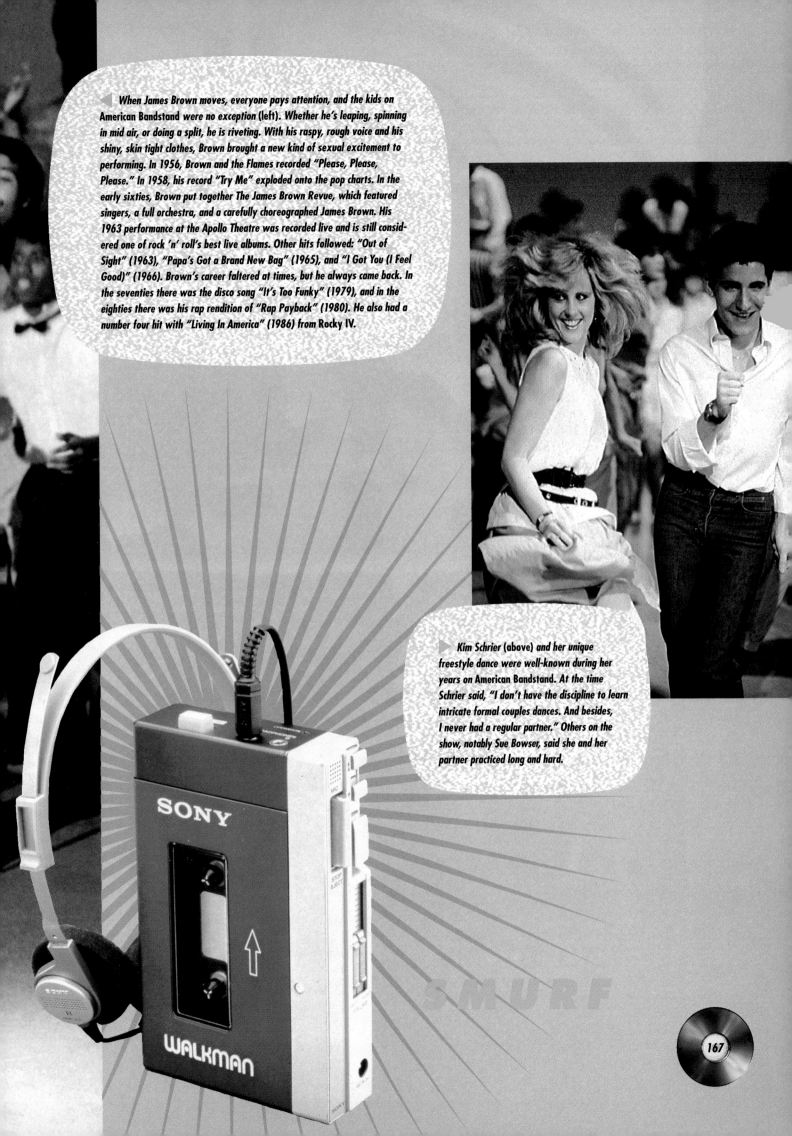

When James Brown moves, everyone pays attention, and the kids on American Bandstand were no exception (left). Whether he's leaping, spinning in mid air, or doing a split, he is riveting. With his raspy, rough voice and his shiny, skin tight clothes, Brown brought a new kind of sexual excitement to performing. In 1956, Brown and the Flames recorded "Please, Please, Please." In 1958, his record "Try Me" exploded onto the pop charts. In the early sixties, Brown put together The James Brown Revue, which featured singers, a full orchestra, and a carefully choreographed James Brown. His 1963 performance at the Apollo Theatre was recorded live and is still considered one of rock 'n' roll's best live albums. Other hits followed: "Out of Sight" (1963), "Papa's Got a Brand New Bag" (1965), and "I Got You (I Feel Good)" (1966). Brown's career faltered at times, but he always came back. In the seventies there was the disco song "It's Too Funky" (1979), and in the eighties there was his rap rendition of "Rap Payback" (1980). He also had a number four hit with "Living In America" (1986) from Rocky IV.

Kim Schrier (above) and her unique freestyle dance were well-known during her years on American Bandstand. At the time Schrier said, "I don't have the discipline to learn intricate formal couples dances. And besides, I never had a regular partner." Others on the show, notably Sue Bowser, said she and her partner practiced long and hard.

Record Review got a new name—Rate-A-Record—soon after the show moved to California. By the seventies and eighties, instead of three kids judging three records, it was down to two judges (above), and Dick Clark did all the math.

Taking advantage of computer technology and deregulation of the airwaves in 1980, Warner Communications launched Music Television, or MTV (above), on August 1, 1981, broadcasting short video clips of rock bands and singers. The first video shown, "Video Killed the Radio Star," by the Buggles, was prophetic; teenagers made the channel a way of life. Suddenly, a band's look was as important as its sound. However, the music video was not altogether new. During Bandstand's early days, the show featured short films of singers and big bands. In the eighties, the music video grew into an art form, creating a visual language that teens related to immediately.

The American Bandstand set of the eighties (above) was television's version of an outer space, glitzy disco. With lights streaming from the ceiling and multi-leveled platforms breaking up the dance floor, the camera found action wherever it pointed.

The eighties was a time of affluence and indulgence, and kids were once again looking for something new. Disco was dying and the fashions it inspired were no longer trendy. Designer clothes were important—Giorgio Armani, Perry Ellis, Ralph Lauren, and Calvin Klein were names every kid knew. Kids also drew inspiration from other eras. Sometimes, the look was modified fifties (left) with preppy white bucks, plaid shirts and jackets, full dresses, bermuda shorts, and espadrilles. Fashion was one of the clearest indications of changing times on American Bandstand from the 1950s to the 1980s. Reflecting the laid-back style and warm weather of Southern California, kids in the eighties were allowed to wear shorts.

MORAL MAJORITY

When American Bandstand began in 1957, the dances the teens did on the show were simple—the same dances they danced in their basements and at local hops. But in the late seventies, disco and a new awareness of media changed dance into performance (opposite). The Hustle was intricate but similar to social dances of the forties and fifties. Eighties dancers, who were raised on television, were more aware of performing for the camera than their fifties counterparts. To look good they rehearsed and planned their moves, giving their dances a polished look.

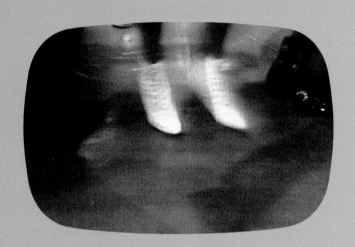

Trained by her brothers, The Jackson 5, Janet Jackson set out on her own in 1982 and became a pop-diva. MTV boosted her popularity when it saturated the air waves with the video from her third album, Control (1986), in which she declares her sexual and social independence, a message that resonated with teens. She appeared on Bandstand (right) in 1987. As American Bandstand was ending its thirty-seven year run on television, Jackson was soaring to new heights with her Rhythm Nation (1989).

Jon Bon Jovi (John Francis Bongiovi) (below), one of the most photogenic pop singers ever, used his good looks to soften the hard edge of his pop-metal band's sound. The group's third album, Slippery When Wet (1986), put it on the musical map. With the savvy of politicians, Bon Jovi's producers had teens rate thirty of the songs being considered for the album. The highest rated made it on to the album, and it sold nine million copies.

174

Cyndi Lauper started out in the early seventies singing back-up with small groups, but her singing style—gruff, high-pitched screams—ruined her voice and she had to work with a voice coach to revive it. With her little-girl rasp and her secondhand clothes, she became the idol of millions of young girls in the early eighties. One of the first stars of the music video revolution, her popularity grew because of her regular appearances in music videos. Her first album, She's So Unusual (1983), was the first by a woman to generate five hit singles. The title of one of them, "Girls Just Want to Have Fun," became an eighties catch phrase.

O Z O N E

Gloria Estefan was the first superstar to come out of Miami's Cuban community. Born in Havana, her family fled Fidel Castro's regime and came to the U.S. in 1959 when she was two years old. In the mid-seventies, she sang in Spanish with the disco-pop salsa group Miami Latin Boys, who changed their name to the Miami Sound Machine. In 1984, they recorded their first English language record "Eyes of Innocence." A year later, they released the English language album Primitive Love, which spawned three hits, including "Conga," setting Estefan and the group on the way to superstardom. In 1987, their Let It Loose album went platinum, and the single "Anything for You" hit number one. The perky, well-groomed Estefan scored big with her English language records, but once established, she began to record again in Spanish, bringing more depth and character to her singing.

177

what we wore

Ankle bracelets	Madras
Army jackets	Maxi skirts
Baggy pants	Miniskirts
Bell bottoms	Mood rings
Bermuda shorts	Muumuus
Bikinis	Nehru jackets
Boatneck shirts	Painter's pants
Chinos	Peacoats
Clogs	Pedal pushers
Culottes	Penny loafers
Dashikis	Perry Como sweaters
Desert boots	Platform shoes
Dickies	Pleated skirts
Down jackets	Ripped jeans
Earth shoes	Sack dresses
Fake fur	Saddle shoes
Felt skirts	Satin pants
Fishnet stockings	Shells
Frye boots	Short shorts
Go-go boots	Skorts
Granny glasses	Spandex
Grunge	Stretch pants
Halter tops	Swatch watches
Headbands	Tank tops
Hip huggers	Tie-dyed t-shirts
Hot pants	Tube tops
Hush puppies	Turtlenecks
Jean jackets	Wedgies
Keds	White bucks
Leg warmers	White lipstick
Leisure suits	White sox
Love beads	Work shirts

The punk movement, which reached its peak in the early eighties, began in New York City's CBGB club as a direct challenge to the excessive corporate rock of the mid-1970s. The music was minimalistic, abrasive, and angry. Richard Hell of the group Television created the punk look—short, spiky hair, ripped t-shirts and jeans, and safety pins everywhere. The Ramones exported the movement to England, where it was especially popular with poor kids in rebellion against the rigidity of the Royal Family and Margaret Thatcher's economic policies. By the 1980s, punk was a big tourist attraction in England, where young people (below) dyed their hair outrageous colors and fashioned it into radical shapes, aiming to shake up the status quo.

When Madonna made her national television debut on American Bandstand in 1984 (above), Dick Clark asked what her ambition was. Her answer, "To rule the world." Madonna has continually pushed the envelope of decency and good taste, but teenage girls have responded to her antics from the beginning. Teen girls emulated her by wearing outrageous outfits with boldly visible undergarments. They even colored their hair according to what Madonna's choice was in any given month. In 1985, Madonna was everywhere. She appeared in two films, Vision Quest and Desperately Seeking Susan, sang on stage with her Virgin Tour, and appeared on MTV. She simultaneously had two songs in the top five, "Crazy for You" and "Material Girl." She also scored with "Angel," "Dress You Up," and the club hit "Into the Groove." A year later, Madonna was at the top of the charts again with "Papa Don't Preach." The controversial song advocated that young unwed mothers keep their babies. Madonna remains a role model and to many of her fans her independent spirit is more important than her music.

Cher has successfully reinvented herself three times. In the sixties, she was a hippie rock singer with her then-husband, Sonny Bono; in the seventies she was a wise-cracking TV comedian prone to wearing outrageous, revealing costumes; and in the eighties, she was a film star. Cher (right) left home at the age of sixteen to be a movie star, but met songwriter Bono and got married. Together they recorded several of his songs, mostly under the names Caesar and Clio. They finally scored with "I Got You Babe" (1965), which went to number one. Later they came back with "The Beat Goes On" (1967). In between, Cher had a hit on her own "Bang Bang (My Baby Shot Me Down)" (1966). After her breakup with Sonny in 1975, it was four years before she hit the charts again with "Take Me Home" (1979). Her acting and singing careers reached high points in the eighties with her 1987 Oscar-winning performance in Moonstruck and her first gold album Cher.

HIJACK

The artist formerly known as Prince made his music debut on American Bandstand in 1980 (opposite). Born in Minneapolis in 1958, Prince Rogers Nelson gained his reputation for lewdness in high school with his band Champagne. His first album, For You (1978), was a unique musical effort in which he played all the instruments. He then scored with the single "I Wanna Be Your Lover" (1979). The subject matter raised a few eyebrows and brought him notoriety. But nothing prepared audiences for his third album, Dirty Mind (1980). Its songs were about sexual discovery and he delivered them in a breathy, sexy manner that left the listener excited and shocked. Initially, Prince's performance attire was also seen as outrageous—he would wear a G-string or nothing at all under a loose-fitting raincoat. Eventually he gave in to modesty by wearing a purple greatcoat and black Lycra jockey shorts. In 1982, he had his first top ten hit, "Little Red Corvette." But when fame finally came, he wanted nothing to do with it. Prince became a recluse at his Minneapolis home, and later dropped his name in favor of a symbol. During his career, Prince has granted few interviews; his only TV interview to date has been with Dick Clark on American Bandstand.

L.L. Cool J (Ladies Love Cool James) was nine years old when he began rapping. At sixteen he recorded his first single "I Need a Beat" (1984), which sold 100,000 copies. Rap, like Breakdancing, came out of the Hip-hop movement in New York's South Bronx. It originated with club deejays, known as spinners, who personalized their segues from one record to another with "raps," or spoken rhythmic rhymes. Using turntables equipped with a special stylus that allowed them to rotate the records back and forth, the deejays created new sounds to accompany their rhymes. With its raw energy and its controversial subject matter, rap harkened back to early rock 'n' roll when songs challenged the safety and emptiness of pop music. Public Enemy's album It Takes a Nation of Millions to Hold Us Back (1988) changed the tone of rap to taunting and hard-hitting. 2 Live Crew and N.W.A. turned from anti-poverty and anti-violence messages to misogyny and revenge. Ironically, the more violent the subject matter, the more suburban white males bought the music.

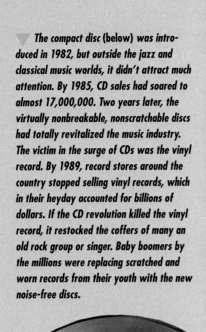

The compact disc (below) was introduced in 1982, but outside the jazz and classical music worlds, it didn't attract much attention. By 1985, CD sales had soared to almost 17,000,000. Two years later, the virtually nonbreakable, nonscratchable discs had totally revitalized the music industry. The victim in the surge of CDs was the vinyl record. By 1989, record stores around the country stopped selling vinyl records, which in their heyday accounted for billions of dollars. If the CD revolution killed the vinyl record, it restocked the coffers of many an old rock group or singer. Baby boomers by the millions were replacing scratched and worn records from their youth with the new noise-free discs.

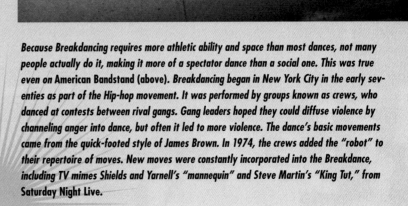

Because Breakdancing requires more athletic ability and space than most dances, not many people actually do it, making it more of a spectator dance than a social one. This was true even on American Bandstand (above). Breakdancing began in New York City in the early seventies as part of the Hip-hop movement. It was performed by groups known as crews, who danced at contests between rival gangs. Gang leaders hoped they could diffuse violence by channeling anger into dance, but often it led to more violence. The dance's basic movements came from the quick-footed style of James Brown. In 1974, the crews added the "robot" to their repertoire of moves. New moves were constantly incorporated into the Breakdance, including TV mimes Shields and Yarnell's "mannequin" and Steve Martin's "King Tut," from Saturday Night Live.

YUPPIES

Acknowledgments

Thanks to Dick Clark and his staff for their support and assistance on *Dick Clark's American Bandstand*. This book would not exist without the participation of Kaydee Meideros, who researched the photographs with diligence and good humor, and Brian Carroll, who participated in interviews and contributed research to the text with enthusiasm and insight into the music business. Bob Chuck made what seemed impossible at times, possible, through his patience and perseverance. Tony Siedl and Fred Bronson helped with matters that pertained to the captions, and Jeff James, Logan Whitechurch, Kari Clark, and Bob Uris solved problems and answered questions along the way.

Ray Smith, who wrote the captions in the book, was an invaluable source of information. His knowledge of *American Bandstand*, which he danced on from 1956 to 1958, and about rock 'n' roll and music in general never ceased to amaze. Thanks to the kids, now grown up, who were regulars on *American Bandstand*: Arlene Sullivan, Myrna Horowitz, Kenny Rossi, Bunny Gibson, Justine Carelli, Carmen Jiminez, Ed Kelly, Carol Scaldeferri, Paul Thomas, Tom DeNoble, and Jimmy Peatross. Thanks also go out to Mark Spergel, Phil Reed, Wes Richards, Vera Badamo, Bea Martin, Tom Martin, Catherine Germano, Lisa Burns, Justin Jackson, Scott Storbo, Mary Deitch, Aurilla Hatcher, Meredith Grappone, Willie Calvert, Bill Levers, Andy Fisher, Lea Whitener Schlobohm, Robert Boyd, Larry Schwartz, Vickie Warren, Ron Ansana of the CNBC The Names Project, Susan Williamson of the Annenberg School of Communications, and Todd Morgan of Graceland. Thanks to Dave Frees, president of The American Bandstand Fan Club, Ephrata, Pennsylvania, for his generosity, knowledge, and great enthusiasm which he so willingly shared. Rosemary Alley, Megan Gannon, Kate Lacey, and Kate Sellar provided research and support at each step. Colleagues at various picture agencies came through as usual. Many thanks to Michael Schulman, Archive Photos; Phillip Reeser, Ernst Haas Archive; Ron and Howard Mandelbaum, Photofest; Jocelyn Clapp, The Bettmann Archive; Kathi Doak, Time-Life Picture Service; Ann Limongello, ABC Photo Archives, who generously made a rich resource available; and Carrie Chalmers, Magnum Photos. Jack Frascatore at Timewarp was generous in providing the period objects that appear throughout the book. Irene Borger helped with valuable research on dance. To Larry Wolfson, Mary Littell and Elizabeth Hansen, appreciation is boundless. Gerry Smith and Dado Feinblatt also made a difference. At Collins, thanks to Melissa Germaine, Liz Sullivan, Sarah Krall, and Renato Stanisic, who worked to capture the spirit of *American Bandstand*.

Photography Credits

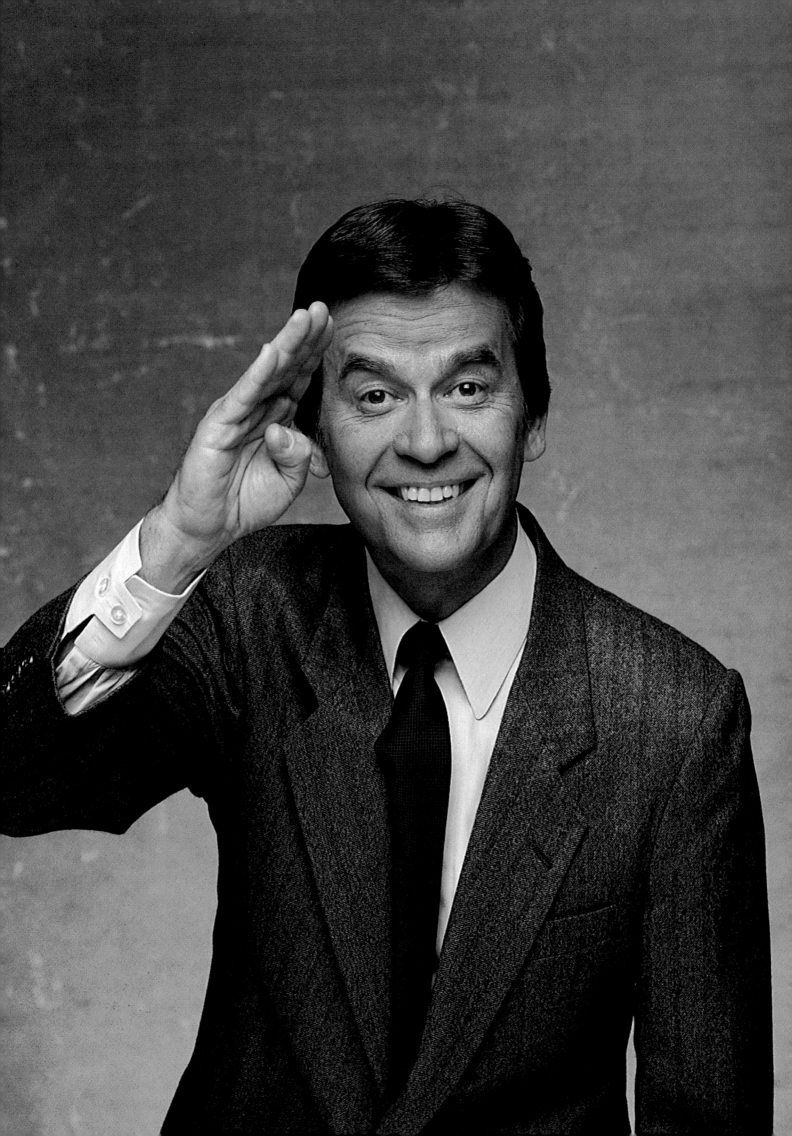

Index

References to photographs and captions are in italics

advertising, 44
AIDS, 154, 155, *155*
American Music Awards, The, 157
Armstrong, Neil, 81
Atlantic City, 21, 97, *96–97*
automobile, 88
Avalon, Frankie, 17, 22, 70, 71, *70–71*, 84, 96, *96*

Baez, Joan, 87, *87*
Bandstand: changes in format, 17, 83, 85, 131, 135, 148, 159–160; changes in production team, 123; changing age of dancers, 122, *142*; dance contests, 46, *46*, 49, *49–50*, 51, *51–52*, 118, *118–119*, 155; dancers on, *10–11, 26–27, 30, 35, 46–47, 56, 58–59, 64–67, 102–104, 110–13, 116–19, 130–34, 143, 146–47, 149, 150–51, 162–65, 167, 169, 170–73, 183–87*; dress code, 19, 61, 91, 111, 122, 171; effect of technology on, 135, 142; fan club, 79; imitation of, 62, *62–63*; move to California, 21, 75, 85, 11, 118, 142; number of shows, 184; Record Review (Rate-A-Record), 15, 16, 21, 49, *49*, 84, 168; Roll Call, 15, 48, *48*; as social experience, 22, 91, 100; Spotlight Dance, 15, 142, *143*, 155, 163, *163*; syndication of, 159
Beach Boys, The, 85, 104
Beals, Jennifer, 154
Beatles, The, 83, 84, 85, 86, 87, 91, 106, 108, *108–9*, 117, *117*, 154, 157, 159, 160
Bee Gees, The, 126, 153
Belafonte, Harry, 19, 156
Berlin wall, *158*, 159
Berry, Chuck, 15, 17, 22, 88
Bobbettes, The, 17, 106
Bogart, Neil and Joyce, 126, 128
Bon Jovi, 157, 174, *174*
Brown, James, *166*, 167
Byrnes, Edd, *100*, 101

Caravan of Stars, 83, 85, 86, 92, *92–93*, 95, 97, *96–97*
Carpenter, Richard and Karen, 125
Carter, Jimmy, 128
Cassidy, Shawn, 125
censorship, 18, 159
Challenger, *152*, 153

Checker, Chubby, 17, 18, 84, 87, 105, *105*
Cher, 180, *180*
civil rights movement, *12*, 13, 20, 124; music of, 87; student protests, 87, 89
Clark, Dick, *8–9, 13, 28–29, 36–37, 42–45, 47–56, 60–61, 64–65, 67–73, 81, 92–93, 96–100, 108–14, 121, 136, 142, 144, 153, 164–65, 168, 186–87, 189*; aging, 142, 159; advertising spokesman, *44–45, 45*; as authority figure, 89; early career, 13, 15; champion of rock 'n' roll, 15; entrepreneur, 29; influence on rock 'n' roll, 14, 19; movie star, 68, 99, *98–99*; 157; popularity of, 68, *68–69*
Cole, Nat King, 13, 126
communism, 15, *15*
compact discs, 183, *183*

dances, 10, 30, 31, 16; Batman, 116; Breakdancing, 154, 182, 183, *183*; Bump, 122; Bunny hop, 64; Calypso, 56; Cha-lypso, 32, 56, *56*; Charleston, 32, 105; Dirty Dancing, 154; Fox Trot, 31; Frug, 122; Funky Chicken, 116; Hip-hop, 147, 182, 183; Hitchhike, 116; Hustle, 122, 162; Jerk, 116, 122; Jitterbug, 30, *30*, 32, 162; Lindy Hop, 32; Monkey, 116; Salsa, 162; Slow Dancing, 66, *66*, 67; Stroll, 31, 32, 64–65, 83, 154; Swim, 116, 122, 154; Swing, 31, 32; Twist, 31, 32, 83, 88, *104, 105, 105*, 116, 122, 147, 154; Waltz, 31
Danny & the Juniors, 17, 18, 20, 36, *36–37*
Darin, Bobby, 17, 88
Dave Clark 5, 84, 85
Dean, James, 73
deejays, 29, 62
Depression, The, 16
Devo, 159
discotheques, 148, *148*, 163
Domino, Fats, 16, 22, 88
Dovells, The, 17, 83
drugs, 87, 89, 91, 108, 117
Duke, Patty, 101, *101*
Dylan, Bob, 87, *87*, 91

Earth Day, *120*, 121
Eisenhower, Dwight David, 13, 82, 83
Estefan, Gloria, 128, *176*, 177
Everly Brothers, The, 15, 38, *38*, 114

Fabian, 17, 70, *70*, 71
fashion, 10, 19, 25, 91, 108, 111, 113, 122, 128, 140, *140*, 148, 154, 162, 171, 178
Faubus, Orval, 13

Four Tops, 84, 86
Francis, Connie, 36, *36*, 60, 84, 104
Franklin, Aretha, 115, *115*
Friedan, Betty, 124
Funicello, Anette, 71, 96, *96*, 100, *100*

Gabriel, Peter, 156
Gaynor, Gloria, 128, 148
Glazer, Barry, 126, 156, 160
Goffin, Gerry, 84, 122
Goldenson, Leonard, 81, 84
Gordy, Berry, 22, 86, 106, *107*, 121
Gore, Lesley, 84, 89, 125
Grateful Dead, 91, 131, 156
Grease, 144
Guns n' Roses, 141

Hair, 25, 56, 75, 91, 111, 135
Haley, Bill, 14, 16, 18, 22
Harris, Oren, 82
Holly, Buddy, 15, 17, 22
homosexuality, 128, 140, 148, 153, 154, 155
Horn, Bob, 13, 20, 47
Hudson, Rock, 154

Iran Contra scandal, 81

Jackson 5, 122, 144, 157, 174
Jackson, Janet, 157, 174, *174–75*
Jackson, Michael, 22, 122, 144, *145*, 153, 159, 160
Jefferson Airplane, 89, 91, 131
John Bartram High School, 36
Johnson, Lyndon, 84

KC & the Sunshine Band, 121, 128
Kennedy, John. F, 82, *82*, 83, 91, 126
Khomeini, Ayatollah, 128, *128*
King, Carole, 60, 84, 122
King, Martin Luther, Jr., 13, 91
Kinks, The, 84, 114, 117
Klein, Larry, 123, 153, 155
Klu Klux Klan, 20

Lauper, Cyndi, 156, 177, *177*
Led Zepplin, 141, *141*
Lee, Brenda, 72, *72–73*
Lennon, John, 154, 159
Levittown, 22, *22*
Lewis, Jerry Lee, 15, 17, 39, *39*, 88
Little Richard (Penniman), 22, 41, *41*
L. L. Cool J, 182, *182*

Madonna, 156, 160, 178, *178–79*
Magazines: *Celebrity*, 69; *Photoplay*, 69; 16, 76; *'Teen*, 76, 78; *TV Guide*, 69
Mamas & the Papas, The, 89
Mammarella, Tony, 13, 14, 15, 16, 17, 18, 19, 20, 38, *38*, 84
Martha & the Vandellas, 86, 106

188

Marvelettes, The, 86, 106
Mathis, Johnny, 17, 49, *49*
McCarthy, Joseph, 15
Mellencamp, John, 153, 155, 156
Metallica, 141
Miracles, The, 86, 106
Miss America, 19
Monkees, The, 88
moon landing, the, 80, *81*
Morrison, Jim, 89
movies: beach movies, 96, *96*; *Beach Party,* *96; Blackboard Jungle,* 22, 99; Dick Clark movies, 99, *98–99, 157;* clean teen movies, 100; *Flashdance,* 154; *Hair,* 142; *Juvenile Jungle,* 73, *73; Moonstruck, 180;* rebel films, 73, *73,* 88; teens in, 100–101; *Saturday Night Fever,* 126, 144, 148, *148; West Side Story,* 111, *111*
Murray, Arthur and Kathryn, 31, *31*
music industry: business of, 18, 43, *43;* early days of, 18; globalization of, 153; influence of MTV, 168, *168;* integration of, 20, 38; social consciousness of, 155, *155, 156, 156,* 183
music, kinds of: disco, 121, 128, 135, 148, *148,* 153, 155, 162, 169, 171; heavy metal, 141; jazz, 86, 88, 115, 183; popular, 14, 34, 86, 88, 115, 155; punk, 155, 159, 178, *178;* rap, 157, 182, *182;* rhythm & blues, 13, 14, 17, 18, 38, 41, 85, 86, 115, 126, 157; soul, 115. *See also* rock 'n' roll.

Nelson, Rick, 101, *101*
Nelson, Willie, 156
Newton, Wayne, 88
Nixon, Richard M., 19, 121, 126, *127*

"101" Strings, 17
Orlando, Tony & Dawn, 87, 136, *136*
Osmond Brothers, 125, 136, *136*

payola hearings, 43, 81, 82
Peterson, Paul, 100, *100*
Philadelphia, 10, 13, 15, 16, 17, 20, 24, 25, 27, 29, 32, 36, 70, *70–71,* 73, 81, 85, 86, 87, 91, 95, 99, 105, 111, 118, 131, 142, 156, 163
Pink Floyd, 49, 159
Platters, The, 38
Presley, Elvis, 15, 22, 40, *41, 83, 91, 106, 160*
Price, Judy, 121, 123
Prince, 22, 155–56, 160, 180, *181*

racial issues, 13, 14, 17, 19, 20, 21, 40, 86, 115, 144
radio, 13, 14, 63, *63,* 167; WDAS, 18; WPEN, 16

Reagan, Ronald, 123, 154
record companies: A&M, 85, 159; Aldon Music, 60; Atlantic Records, 115; Cadence, 38; Cameo-Parkway, 18, 70, 88; Capitol Records, 84; Casablanca Records, 126; Chancellor Records, 71; Essex Records, 17; Memphis Recording Service, 40; Motown, 22, 86, 106, *107,*144; Singular Records, 18, 36; Sun Records, 40; Swan Records, 84; T. K. Records, 128; Vee Jay records, 18
records, 183; 45 RPM, 29, 117; 78 RPM, 29, 47, 63
Reddy, Helen, 124, 125, 128
regulars, 15, 21, 30, 33, 34, 36, 50, 75, *74–75,* 78, *78–79,* 83, 95, 111, 123, 164; Badama, Vera, 24; Balara, Mike, 52, *52–53;* Blyth, Linda, 155; Bowser, Sue, 167; Carelli, Justine, 21, 35, *35,* 78, *78;* Contreras, Johnny, 154–55; Clayton, Bob, 21, 35, 78, *78,* 79; De Noble, Tom, 75; DeSera, Lou, 25, *25;* Freeman, Damita Jo, 122; Gibson, Bunny, 33, 75; Giordano, Frani, 52, *52–53;* Hooks, Famous, 21; Horowitz, Myrna, 33; Jimenez, Carmen, 52, *52–53,* 56, *56–57, 76–77,* 79; Jimenez, Ivette, 56, *56–57, 76–77;* Kelly, Ed, 75; Kerr, Norman, 53, *52–53;* Marcen, Barbara, 33; Molittieri, Pat, 30, *30,* 77; MonteCarlo, Carmen, 24, *24;* Rosney, David, 128; Rossi, Kenny, 21, 33, 34, *34;* Scaldeferri, Carole, 33; Schaeffer, Joyce, 52, *52–53;* Schrier, Kim, 167, *167;* Sullivan, Arlene, 21, 33, 34, *34,* 56; Vacca, Frank, 52, *52–53;* Zamil, Charlie, 24, *24*
Richie, Lionel, 157
rock concerts, 87, 156, *156*
rock 'n' roll: concept albums, 117; British invasion, 84, 85, 111, 155; early days of, 13, 18, 29; girl groups, 106, 107; industry of, 14, 106; influence of blacks on, 13, 86, 115, 144; origins of, 13, 14; protest songs, 89, 115, 124, 128; provoking riots, 34, *34;* reactions against, 13, 14, 15,19, 82; success of, 82; synthesizer sound of, 135, 148, 155
Rolling Stones, The, 114
Ross, Diana, 92, *93,* 106, *106–7,* 121, 122
Rydell, Bobby, 17, 18, 70, *70,* 83, 84

Sedaka, Neil, 60, *60,* 125
Sharp, Dee Dee, 17, 84
Shirelles, The, 86, 122
Sinatra, Frank, 16, 61
Singer, Artie, 18, 36

Studio 54, 148
Summer, Donna, 128, 135, *135*
Supreme Court, 13, 123
Supremes, The, 84, 86, 91, 106, *106–07,* 121
Swayze, Patrick, 154

teenagers: as advertising market, 44; civil rights activity, 13; as consumers, 24, 73, 104; environmentalists, 121; fads, 24, 88, *88,* 108, 154; fans, 79, 108; hippies, 89, *90,* 91, 131; innocence of, 18; juvenile delinquents, 19, 73; rebellion of, 34, *34,* 91
Telestar, 81
television: ABC, 16, 17,19, 21, 81, 89, 91, 121, 153, 154, 159; awareness of media, 171; coverage of Kennedy assassination, 82; early days of, 16, 67; medium of, 10, 87, 150, 164; MTV, 144, 168, *168,* 174, 178; NBC, 114; RCA, 16; rock 'n' roll on, 14; sets in America, 16; shows for teens, 15, 27; videotaping, 153; WFIL, 10, 13, 15, 16, 21, 78, 81
television programs: *Adventures of Ozzie and Harriet,* 100, 101; *Amos 'n' Andy,* 16; *Brady Bunch,* 138, *138–39; Burns & Allen,* 16; *Cosby Show,* 100; *Donna Reed Show,* 83, 100; *Father Knows Best,* 83, 100; *Hullabaloo,* 114; *Jack Benny,* 16; *Mickey Mouse Club,* 100; *My Three Sons,* 100; *Our Miss Brooks,* 16; *Shindig,* 114, *114; Sunset Strip,* 101; *Twenty-One,* 43; *Welcome Back, Kotter,* 126, 144; *X-Files,* 81
Temptations, The, 86, 91
Thatcher, Margaret, 178
Thompson, Hunter, 91
Three Dog Night, 91, 121
Travolta, John, 126, 144, *144,* 148, *148*
Truman, Harry S, 83

Van Debur, Marilyn, 19
Van Doren, Charles, 43
videos, music, 153, 168, 174, 177
Vietnam, 84, *84,* 89, 91, 121, 123
Village People, 128, 140, *140–41*
Vinton, Bobby, 84, 136

Watergate, 81, 126
Wells, Mary, 84, 86
Whiskey-A-Go-Go, 88
Williams, Andy, 17, 136
Wilson, Jackie, 17, 22
women's movement, 124, 125, 128; in music, 36, 122, 125, 128, 157
World War II, 16, 22, 32, 73

DICK CLARK'S AMERICAN BANDSTAND. Copyright ©
1997 by dick clark productions, inc. All rights reserved.
Printed in the U.S.A. No part of this book may be used
or reproduced in any manner whatsoever without written
permission except in the case of brief quotations embodied
in critical articles and reviews.

For information address:

Collins Publishers
10 East 53rd Street
New York, NY 10022

HarperCollins books may be purchased for educational, business, or sales promotional use.

For information please write:

Special Markets Department
HarperCollins Publishers
10 East 53rd Street
New York, NY 10022

Packaged by Lookout
1024 Avenue of the Americas
New York, NY 10018
212-221-6463

FIRST EDITION

97 98 99 00 01 10 9 8 7 6 5 4 3 2 1

Library of Congress Cataloging-in-Publication Data

Clark, Dick
      Dick Clark's American Bandstand/by Dick Clark:
      [with Fred Bronson].
                    p.   cm.
      ISBN 0-00-649184-7. — ISBN 0-06-757456-4 (pbk.)
      1. American Bandstand (Television program)
      2. Popular music—United States.
      3. Rock music—United States.
      I. Bronson, Fred.
      II. Title.
ML3477.C57 1997   96-45007
791.45'72—dc20   MN